RAFLE
Research Academy for Foreign Language Examinations
朗阁海外考试研究中心
Since 1999

朗阁IELTS应试系列

雅思精品系列教程

IELTS

雅思精品

张月 梁一晓 活玮靖 编著

口语

上海交通大學出版社
SHANGHAI JIAO TONG UNIVERSITY PRESS

内容提要

本书针对报考雅思考试的考生，根据最新的雅思官方口语评分标准，深入剖析每个考点并给出细致的解析。为了让考生真正掌握，本书的每个章节都配有直击考点的练习，让考生的口语练习不再是机械的记忆背诵，也达到显著的提分效果。

图书在版编目(CIP)数据

雅思精品口语／张月，梁一晓，活玮靖编著. —上海：上海交通大学出版社，2017(2018重印)
ISBN 978-7-313-16006-5

Ⅰ. ①雅… Ⅱ. ①张… ②梁… ③活… Ⅲ. ①IELTS—口语—自学参考资料 Ⅳ. ①H319.9

中国版本图书馆CIP数据核字(2016)第269643号

雅思精品口语

编　　著：张　月　梁一晓　活玮靖
出版发行：上海交通大学出版社　　地　　址：上海市番禺路951号
邮政编码：200030　　电　　话：021-64071208
出 版 人：谈　毅
印　　制：常熟市文化印刷有限公司　　经　　销：全国新华书店
开　　本：787 mm×1092 mm　1/16　　印　　张：11
字　　数：248千字
版　　次：2017年1月第1版　　印　　次：2018年2月第3次印刷
书　　号：ISBN 978-7-313-16006-5/H
定　　价：49.00元

总　序

朗阁海外考试研究中心（Research Academy for Foreign Language Examinations，简称RAFLE）成立于1999年，是朗阁教育集团旗下的专业学术机构，是针对各类海外语言考试及教学进行系统性研究的专业研发机构。RAFLE研发团队拥有上百位资深中外研究人员，他们遍布全国36个大中型城市，并长期活跃在雅思、新托福、SAT、ACT、GRE、GMAT、TOEFL Junior、SSAT等各大教学领域，对提升朗阁教育集团整体教学水平和研发实力起着重要的作用。

雅思精品阶段系列丛书是由朗阁海外考试研究中心的资深研究员老师通过多年一线教学经验的总结，结合雅思考试的最新趋势所创作出的一套适合雅思考生备考的实用系列教材。该套教材旨在帮助中国考生熟悉、适应和从容应对雅思考试中各种题型的特点，了解和熟悉最新雅思考试的趋势和难点，掌握并灵活运用必要的考试技巧，提高应试能力。书中的内容讲练结合，难度贴近考试，适合具有大二、大三英语程度，已通过大学英语四级考试，英语基础较为扎实，但对雅思缺乏明确认识的考生。学习完该系列教程及相关课程，考生可以达到雅思6分及以上水平。

本系列丛书由朗阁海外考试研究中心教材编写团队共同制作完成。编写团队深谙雅思官方的出题思路，对教材的定位、全书的框架结构、重点难点、题目、解析及答案、精品系列与其他系列教材之间的通路等各个方面都进行了深入细致的探讨。教材从拟写草稿到初稿，再到后面的二稿和定稿，编写团队的老师们经过反复推敲，最终确定了最适合最实用的版本。

本书在使用的过程中，学生可以根据教材的章节顺序进行学习，也可根据自己的实际情况进行调整：

雅思精品系列的听力书，针对雅思听力题型多样性的特点和难点，以雅思听力题型为主线，对各题型的题型特点与核心技巧进行全面深入的总结和剖析，并基于研发中心对于雅思听力考试长期不懈的追踪，为考生抽丝剥茧，整理出最精准、最高效的解题方法步骤。

考生只要按照书中的要求训练和备考，一定可以融会贯通、取得优异的听力成绩，同时大大提升自身的听力能力。

阅读书由十个章节组成。第一章是雅思阅读简介。其中讲解了雅思阅读的题型介绍和技巧汇总，而且列出了相关的技能提高小贴士。第二章到第九章是雅思阅读题型技能训练，分析了雅思主流题型的题目特点和应试技巧，并辅以相关的文章训练，使学生掌握所有题型的应试方法。第十章是雅思阅读测试（学术类和普通培训类）。这章中的所有文章和题型设置，均参照最新雅思阅读考试的特点，从文章和题目的难度到各种题型所占比例，完全符合雅思考试的特点，尽可能还原雅思阅读考试的特点，而且考虑到学生类和普通培训类考生的不同需求，我们编排了两类练习。

写作对 A 类考生来说，建议大小作文交叉着学习。小作文练习熟练度很重要，但是四种类型一起学，难免效率会低下，所以建议交叉学。对 G 类考生来说，建议将 70% 的时间花在大作文方面，信件类文章相对简单，但要熟悉常用表达。

口语教材涵盖了雅思口语几乎所有的常考话题。针对每一类话题，本书中都有相应的高分范文和解析，并配有相应的练习题、小贴士和话题词汇。此外，本书还配有雅思口语的评分标准，以及6.5 分水平的考生案例，供同学们参考。同学们可以根据目录来查找相应的雅思口语话题。朗读高分范文，并在老师的指导下分析范文。然后完成练习题，并背诵话题词汇。

本系列教材的主要编写者有：贾若寒、曹燕、王华、张月、梁一晓、赵瑜斌、曹美玲、活玮靖、李赫。在此谨向各位老师致以最衷心的感谢！

朗阁海外考试研究中心

2016.10.9

目　录

Chapter 1 Introduction

一、雅思口语考试简介

考试时间：11－14 分钟

口语考试将会有一位经过培训的考官参与，并且考试全程会有录音。

Part	Time	What will I need to talk about?
1	4－5 minutes	Questions on familiar topics (e. g. hobbies, likes and dislikes, etc.). 熟悉的生活话题问答
2	3－4 minutes	You will be given a booklet with a topic (e. g. describe a good friend) and some suggestions. You need to talk about the topic for 1－2 minutes. You have about one minute to write notes before you begin. 话题卡：你会看到一张话题卡，并且有一分钟的时间思考做笔记，回答时间为 1—2 分钟。
3	4－5 minutes	The examiner will ask you more detailed and more abstract questions about the topic in Part 2 (e. g. How important is friendship?). 考官会就第二部分话题卡的话题问一些延伸的，更为细节或者抽象的问题。

二、雅思(IELTS)口语考试评分标准和 3 个考试部分(Part 1,2,3)的历史来源

雅思口语考试的评分标准从流利度与连贯性，词汇运用，语法，发音与语音四个方面考查考生。2001 年 7 月以前的雅思口语考试只有一个总分数，而这个总分数是考官对这个考生的印象而已。虽然考官也是有参考上述的四个评分标准来测评考生的口语水平，但是只是粗略的估计，给出总体的印象分数。改革后的评分标准要求在流利与连贯、词汇、语法、发音和语音四个方面考察考生，并分项量化，每项分别给出分数(subscore)，然后将四个分数折算成最后的一个总分数(Band score)。

而在 2001 年新评分标准出现后，为了配合当时的新评分标准，还有另一项重大改变，也就是**考官规范(Examiner frame)机制**的使用。这个考官规范是为考官制定雅思口语考试发问问题的数量、范围，和考官自己与考生对话中扮演的角色有明确的书面规定。考

官在口试的 Part 1 和 Part 2 中使用的语言和使用的问题都被严格控制(直接从 Examiner frame 里面的 Examiner question bank 中直接念出题目),以确保所有考生以同样的规格接受统一难度的提问。在 Part 3, Examiner frame 相对宽松,考官可以根据学生的程度和表现挑选问题,也可以适当调整自己的语言(paraphrase)以让问题更切合考生的理解能力。但整体来说,改革后的雅思口语考试的流程、谈话内容和形式以及评分标准被严格规定,考官评分标准更为客观。

因此,在某种程度上,一个语法弱、词汇不是太丰富、发音较差但是善于沟通、讲话相对流利的考生,如果按照改革前的标准能得 6 分的话,改革后新评分标准里,这位考生可能只拿到 5 分或更低。这是因为改革前的考试谈话自由度较大,当中有较多的双向沟通,考官评分的主观成分较高;而改革后的四个评分标准都要分项量化打分,考官的侧重转移到学生的口语技术层面上,如时态的标准、用词是否多元化而准确等方面。这样的评分结果也能更客观地反映考生的实质英语口语语言水平。

三、现行的四个评分标准及内容

雅思口语考试的四项评分标准如下:

流利度与连贯性—Fluency and Coherence (FC)

词汇运用—Lexical Resource (LR)

语法、文法准确性与能力—Grammar Range and Accuracy(GRA)

发音与语音—Pronunciation (Pr)

四项评分标准按照 1 到 9 分,共分 9 个等级。只要考生出席口语考试,就能拿到四项评分标准 1 分的成绩,换句话说,考生只要进入考场,说声 Hello,坐在考官面前确认个人信息,就能拿到最低分数。如果考生想拿每一项评分标准的 9 分,就需要能够灵活和准确地运用该单项里要求的技巧。需要注意的是,每项评分标准的分数等级是没有小数点的整数,也就是说,考生某一评分单项可能是 5 分、6 分、7 分而绝对不会是 5.5 分或 6.5 分。但是,四项评分加起来后再得出一个平均分后,是能出现小数点的总分数。我们一起来看看一些例子:

考生 A: FC 7 分 + LR 6 分 + GRA 6 分 + Pr 7 分 = 总分 6.5 分

考生 B: FC 5 分 + LR 5 分 + GRA 5 分 + Pr 6 分 = 总分 5.25 分→5.5 分(雅思口语考试只有整数和 0.5 分的总分,其他分数都会往上或者往下调到最近的 0.5 分数或者整数分数)

流利和连贯程度(Fluency and Coherence)

流利度是指话语的顺畅程度。基本要求的是要连续、不费力地谈话。如果考生是说一句,停一下重新开始,或者回答问题时断断续续,常常挣扎寻找词汇,无法给考官留下流利的印象,就不能说是流畅。因此,只要不招致误解,**出现错误的时候也不用常常回头去修正,做好的办法是保持流畅性继续说下去。**

与此同时,我们必须要说一下考生的两个错误观念——"流利就是语速快","流利就是准确度高"。先回应第一个观念,在不影响语音清晰(Clarity)的前提下,语速偏快是可接受的。**但是如果牺牲语言的清晰度和该有的思考时间(Thinking time)为了语速快,反**

而会让考生得不偿失。保持语速和语调均匀，顺畅是很重要的而缺乏速度控制会让语调忽高忽低，显得不自然。

至于第二个观念，一般来说，考生只要能连续而不费力地进行对答和谈话，流利度也能拿到不错的分数。能脱口而出（Spontaneous）是最好，但是很多考生要思考一下才开始说话，一边说一边组织语言，这在考官的眼里也是正常的。因此，**放慢语速是可以让自己组织语言，控制情绪，这会给考官一种沉稳而有条理的印象**。值得注意的是，很多考生的回答时候太注重自己的语言准确度和语言，导致回答速度过慢，每个字都是重读。这让考官听起来很吃力而且不是英语为母语人士的说话方式。

连贯性是对考生想表达的内容以适当的逻辑组织的特定要求。它具有两方面。第一是指语意关联，也就是考生回答问题不能答非所问，颠三倒四，偏题；而应该紧扣主题，前后连贯，以达到语意上的连接。第二是指语言形式上的连贯，能适当运用连接词来表达多层次的观点，适当运用转折对比等手段来表现话语中的结构。也就是说，考生所表达的句子之间在意义上的关联，顺序符合逻辑，语言结构合理。

评分标准——考生要诀（流利度）

	Do's 该做的（到达这个分数）	Don'ts 不该做的（避免更低分）
Band 5（5 分）	• 碰到什么情况都继续说话。 • 利用简单连接词和口语词。 • 保证简单句子的流利度；有基本而准确的逻辑回答思维。	• 出现不必要和长时间的停顿。 • 过多而错误使用的“口语词（er, um, uh）”。 • 只用简单句型；缺乏链接词；缺乏逻辑。
Band 6（6 分）	• 主动和有能力的（速度、反应）给出不同长度的回答。 • 善用不同的连接词和口语次；但是有时欠缺准确运用。 • 保持一定的回答连贯性；但有时因为过于停顿，自我改正，重复词汇而失去连贯性。	• 回答时候过慢导致答案速度不自然。 • 过度使用连接词和转折词（模板式的）。 • 太多自我改正和自我重复。 • 跳跃式思维，逻辑空乏，说法不连贯。
Band 7（7 分）	• 自然而流畅的回答所有问题；速度把控良好。 • 能使用多元化的连接词和口语词并且能准确使用。 • 良好的连贯性；甚少出现逻辑性错误。 • 允许“想不到单词但是能描述”的停顿。	• 停顿，迟疑，或突然不知所措。 • 出现不自然的语速（太快或太慢）。 • 不愿意发展自己想法和意见；回答逻辑性偏表面。

词汇运用和准确度（Lexical Resource）

词汇运用和准确度指的是考生的词汇多样性和表达能力——词能达意；遇到想不到某些词汇时，能找其他相关的词汇，较少重复用词。在这方面也是有两个指标来衡量：第一是用词得体，适当准确；第二是用词的丰富性——会用**代名词、同义词及描述性词汇**来表达相关概念，而不是干巴巴地重复使用某一些词汇或词组。比如，使用 participate in sporting activities 就可以避免 play sports 或 do sports 的重复。此外，考生是应该用大部分人都知道简单明了词汇，还是用一些相当专业的生僻词汇呢？其实雅思口语考试中，考官无从了解考生到词汇量究竟有多大，而且事实上没有这个必要。考官可以从考生用到词汇是否准确，是否重复使用一些单词来检验考生的词汇量以及考生运用词汇表达思想的能力。

很多学生都追求使用“高大上”的词汇来拉高自己的分数。其实**雅思口语考试当中应该多使用自然容易懂（Natural and Understandable）的词汇和词组**。用词失误比文法失误更造成考官的理解障碍。因此，在一定的意义上，对词汇的把握比对文法规则的把握更重要。**说话时应尽量做到可理解，可听懂，可接受**。尽量不要使用一些自己不太明白怎么用的专业术语或者“高大上”词汇。不会用英语表达时可以透过解释、举例以及身体语言等方式绕个弯说明。

评分标准——考生要诀（词汇）

	Do’s 该做的	Don’ts 不该做的
Band 5	• 能谈论熟悉和不熟悉的话题，但是灵活性有限。 • 回答中尝试运用不同词汇但是欠缺准确性。 • 尝试同义替换但是成功率偏低。	• 过多使用简单词汇。 • 重复使用词汇；不能用不同词汇回答不同的话题。 • 使用不了解的“高大上”词汇导致答案缺乏准确性。
Band 6	• 有足够的词汇谈论各种话题。 • 词汇运用大致准确，能表达基本思路；包含一些使用不当的词。 • 基本能成功地同义替换。	• 不停重复使用错误的同意替换词 • 依赖表情、动作和手势来表达想法。
Band 7	• 能准确并且灵活地使用多元化的词汇来回答各种话题。 • 使用一些非常见词汇、习语/里语、口语化的词汇。 • 有效的同义替换。	• 出现不当词汇，影响对回答的理解。 • 不能灵活运用不同复杂程度的词汇；出现过于复杂和过于简单的回答。 • 回答过于写作化；回答不像自然口语对答。

文法的范围与准确性（Grammar range and accuracy）

口语对答和交流目的在于沟通。文法结构正确和适当的语句比文法错误多的语句会使沟通更畅顺。很多考生往往以为自己对英语文法规则有很深的了解，然而出口更错。问题在于，他们所熟悉的是文法知识和规则，可是在真实沟通中却不知如何运用。这当然不是说忘记语法规则，而是在传统的中式教育下，缺乏真正能使用的场景和机会。

毫无疑问,对于非母语人士的考生而言,文法错误在所难免。考官不会苛求。他们所关注的是文法错误对理解所产生的影响,信息交流是否受阻碍。如果考生的文法错误造成了了解的障碍或影响沟通的顺畅进行,考生在语法评分单项就不能取得比较高的分数。此外,**重复最基础的语法错误也是不能容忍的**,例如 he 说成 she, I am 说成 I is, I like reading books 说成 I very very like read books,等等。考生应尽量避免重复性和习惯性的错误,因这种错误会给考官留下不良印象,直接影响最终分数。

因此,考生展示自己的文法运用能力很重要。在考试时,考官都会仔细听词组和句子的组织及考生是否运用了正确的结构。他们会对考生是否能运用大量不同的句子结构表达自己很感兴趣。比如说,考官想知道考生是否能运用简单结构和复杂结构,而在合适的时候交叉使用。考官还想知道考生对动词时态、名词单复数以及主词与动词一致等文法规则运用的准确度。

评分标准——考生要诀(语法)

* 复杂结构包含:

- 长难句(使用不同连接词): because, but, although, so,等等。
- 语法结构: Conditional(条件句)、Relative Clause(从句),等等。

	Do's 该做的	Don'ts 不该做的
Band 5	• 准确的基本句型。 • 尝试使用复杂句型但是欠缺准确度,影响理解。	• 基本句型出现明显错误(单词过去式不加 ed 或错误加 ed,单词复数不加 s 或者错误加 s)。 • 只使用简单而基本句型;没有出现任何复杂句型。
Band 6	• 使用一定数量的准确基本和复杂句型但是重复性大。 • 复杂句型里的错误不是太严重,不影响理解。	• 基本句和复杂句出现过多的小错误。 • 每几句出现少量的时态、单复数、he/she 分不清的错误,影响理解。
Band 7	• 准确并灵活使用不同种类的复杂结构。 • 虽然句子偶尔有些小错误但是大部分句子都是准确无误。	• 重复使用相同的文法结构。 • 过于注重文法复杂性,答案欠缺自然对答的感觉并牺牲流利度。

发音和语音(Pronunciation)

在发音和语音方面的要求是能使对方听清楚,发音不阻碍理解,每一个词的准确发音都是这项评分标准的依据和标准。这一标准看起来挺简单,但是它是沟通成功的基本前提。有相当一部分考生都存在比较明显的发音问题。这些考生在其他三项评分标准的分数都可能有一定水平,但是因为存在核心的语音问题使得考生拿到的分数都是偏低的。要想使自己的语音得到较大的改善就必须要长时间接触英语,模仿和训练基础的口语发音技巧。考生应熟悉语音基本原则和规律来进行朗读和口语训练,考生定能在英语发音方面获得突破。

当然这并不代表考生不能使用带口音的英语。首先,雅思官方没有统一要求的"标准口音",考生没有必要非得模仿英国的标准英语(Received Pronunciation)或标准美音。考官是允许考生有微微口音的,只要不影响理解,什么口音都可以。

评分标准——考生要诀(发音)

* 发音特点包含:Contraction(惯性缩词)、Weakened Form(弱化音)、Sound links(连音)、Strong form/Weak form(重读、轻化)、Sentence stress(句子重音),等等。

	Do's 该做的	Don'ts 不该做的
Band 5	• 尝试使用发音特点但是出现一定偏差。 • 考官大致能辨别回答中的意思;但是需要仔细分辨才能听懂。	• 口音过重导致理解相当困难。 • 没有使用任何发音特点。 • 将词汇分开,间断地说出来(像念书),非常不自然。
Band 6	• 使用多种发音特点;但是欠缺掌握;不能持续使用。 • 发音大致正确,考官能理解回答中的意思;偶尔出现发音不准确导致清晰度下降。	• 音调单调而没有高低起伏,显得有点不自然。 • 口音或单词发音让考官感觉有压力或者困惑。
Band 7	• 能掌握和持续使用多种发音特点;回答自然。 • 口音没用造成任何回答理解的影响。 • 回答清晰,速度明快,有抑扬顿挫。	• 交流顺畅但是口音偶尔影响理解。 • 回答时速度保持一致(太慢,或太快),没有速度变化。

Chapter 2 Study & Work

话题词汇热身训练

Module 1 词汇

◇ Exercise 1. Make the following into sentences and read the sentences aloud. 用下列单词组成句子并大声朗读。

n.	*v.*	*adj.*
field ambition reputation senior sophomore facility workload budget salary colleague supervisor assignment orientation atmosphere uniform research presentation intern mindset stage	plan graduate analyze move on hesitate get used to focus on have access to consult tackle figure out stand out distinguish inspire evaluate highlight	prestigious troublesome challenging tough stable decent repetitive responsible strict compulsory professional mindful exhausting specific dull

1. I/sophomore/plan to/study abroad/master's.

Example：I'm a sophomore student and I'm planning to study abroad for my master's.

2. His/salary/decent/among/peers.

3. I/like/school/workload/way too heavy.

4. Orientation/held/hall/tomorrow/everyone/attend.

5. Her presentation/focus on/brand-new/field/inspire/me.

◇ Exercise 2. Write down some words or phrases that you can think of within 30 seconds to answer these questions. And then work in pairs to ask and answer these questions. 流利度达成——30 秒内写出你能想到的可以回答下列问题的单词或词组！并与你身边的同学两人一组互相提问回答这些问题。

1. What were some of the most popular activities at primary school?

2. Do you work or are you a student?

3. Do you like your school?

4. How do you improve your efficiency?

5. Do you like to work or study with others or just by yourself?

直击考点

Module 1 Connectives 连接词

Reason & result

Join the first part of a sentence in the left-hand column with a second part from the right-hand column, using an appropriate expression showing reason or result from the central column. In some cases, more than one of the expressions from the middle is possible.

1. The police asked him his ...	... owning to	... pass his exams
2. He failed his exam ...	... so as not to ...	... wake anyone
3. He spent the whole weekend revising ...	... with the aim of ...	... his lack of revision

续表

4. They came in quietly ...	... in order to ...	... poor student attendance
5. The bank manager refused to lend the company more money ...	... due to ...	... its low turnover and poor sales history
6. The school was forced to close ...	... reason for ...	... speeding through the town

Module 2 Paraphrase 词群同义转换

◇ Write down the synonyms of the following words and describe the word to your group members. 写出下列单词的同义词，并用自己话向身边的同学描述这个单词。

Example：hard：tricky，difficult，frustrating，tough，challenging

✓ something not easy and may require a lot of efforts

Interesting：Something not boring and may make people happy

Smart：

Teacher：

Lesson：

Part 1 Interview

Module 1 Evaluate 如何做出评价

雅思口语的 Part 1 中有很多的一般疑问句（General Questions），其中有一些问题会让考生关于一个 opinion 回答自己的评价。例如：

1. Do you think your job is easy? Why?
2. Do you think history is important?
3. Do you think the dictionary is useful?

STEP ONE

回答这些问题时，首先我们需要先对问题做出回应。也就是告诉考官你的答案是

YES or NO。很多考生在考试时没有做出直接的回应，并且在接下来的解释时又含糊不清，会让考官觉得你的思路不够清晰，影响分数。让我们来看下面这一组答案。

Do you think your job is easy? Why?

考生 A：hmm my job is accounting because I learned this major at university, and I think it's very difficult. We have to do many financial statement and statistical analysis.

考生 B：Definitely not. I'm doing accounting right now. Frankly I feel a bit regretful choosing this major at uni, coz it's not just mentally challenging but exhausting. The most horrible thing is we often work overtime. I can't take this. We have to do countless financial statement and statistical analysis every day. I think I'll quit from this job sooner or later.

考生 A 没有直接给出自己的答案，答案也过短，没有体现出 willing to speak at length. 在流利度和词汇上拿不到 6 分。接下来，我们学习一组关于 YES/NO 的口语替换说法，这些表达既口语化也很地道。

Yes	No
Definitely. Absolutely. Certainly. Yep. No doubt. Indeed.	Certainly not. Nope. Not really. Not at all. I'm afraid not.

STEP TWO

有了 yes/no 的回答接下来，我们就针对题目的内容进一步做出**具体的评价**。

Personally, I find it easy in the first place.

In my opinion, this job is quite tough but interesting.

I totally agree with the point that doing a job that you have interests on is more important than your pay.

As far as I know, most engineers are living under high pressure.

As far as I'm concerned, it is never a difficult job.

在雅思口语的 part 1 中大家一定要多说，因此我们还可以进一步**解释**自己对于话题的评价。

My view is, doing something challenging at one's 20 s is meaningful.

In other words, our workload is acceptable.

What I'm trying to say is, I have a flexible working schedule.

By this I mean, my job is ideal and I feel lucky to work in this field.

To be more specific, my job is acceptable at this stage, not perfect for sure and not that bad.

Let me put this in another way, if I was given a second chance I won't choose this company I'm afraid.

◇ Exercise. Answer the following questions. 回答下列问题。

1. Do you think history is important?

2. Do you think the dictionary is useful?

3. Do you think the internet is a good way to learn about history?

Module 2 实战演练

➢ Examiner: Do you use dictionary?

Yep. I use dictionary nearly every day. I installed two or three dictionary apps in my mobile phone like Merriam-Webster and Oxford. Oh I have Youdao too. Though it was complained by my English teacher for countless times, I still find it convenient and handy.

➢ Examiner: Do you think science is important?

Certainly. Science is quite important in terms of both every-day life and social development. For example, what we are using right now such as mobile phones and computers are existing because of science. Without scientific research, modern transportation and medication won't progress.

➢ Examiner: How do you go to school?

Well in fact I'm currently studying in a boarding school, so basically my parents send me by car every Sunday and bring me back home on Friday. Our campus is a bit far away from downtown. And it takes me about two hours to get there by bus. Plus I need to carry some clothes and snacks with me.

➢ Examiner: Do you think computers might one day replace handwriting?

Not really. I think we will still write by hand. I think it's an important skill, and schools will continue to teach children to write by hand before they learn to type. Besides, there are some occasions hand writing is more respectful such as when writing an invitation. At least you need to write postcards on your own, right?

➢ Examiner: Do you think English is difficult to learn?

Kind of. To be honest, the most frustrating part must be vocabulary. It's hard to remember those academic vocabularies and spoken language is not a small piece of cake as well. You know, sometimes you just feel like black out and can't utter anything.

➢ Examiner: Do you like math?

Nope. Not at all. I'm terrible at math. I guess I lack the numerical ability. I can't do those calculations and equations and stuff. I'm more of an art subject person. That's why I chose education as my major for uni.

➢ Examiner: Is it important to focus on things?

Most likely yes. Without an ability to focus on things, one's efficiency could be really low. And that's killing for some specific occasions such as when you are driving. According to the reports, many severe traffic accidents happened due to distraction.

Discourse Markers

我们在看美剧或英剧时,会听到以英语为母语的人士(Native speakers)在说话时常常会用到 discourse markers,例如:"oh","well","now","then","you know"。在英国等国家的大学课堂上,教授也经常在课堂上用到一些 discourse markers,例如:

Well today **I'm gonna** talk about some ways plants defend themselves. **Now**, some plants have physical features that prevent insects from landing on them.

考生在雅思口语考试中掌握这些口语词,会使你的回答更加地道、连贯,是加分必备技能。

Module 3 练习

1. Is there anything about science that you dislike?

2. Do you think learning language is important?

3. Do you like science?

4. What was your favorite subject in secondary school?

5. What language do you speak?

6. How did you learn English?

7. Do you have a favorite teacher?

8. Do you want to be a teacher in the future?

9. Do you think teachers should be angry at students or not?

10. What's the difference between young and old teachers?

11. When did you start learning math?

12. Who taught you math?

13. Who's your favorite teacher so far?

14. Is math difficult for you to learn?

15. When do people need to focus?

16. Is it easy to concentrate on things?

17. Can people focus on two different things at the same time?

18. When was the last time you worked with a team?

19. What's the most important thing for teamwork?

20. Do you like to be a leader?

21. Do you think handwriting is very important (nowadays)?

Part 2 The Long-turn

Module 1 Brainstorming 头脑风暴

◇ Read the examples of a brainstorming exercise. 请看以下头脑风暴的例子。

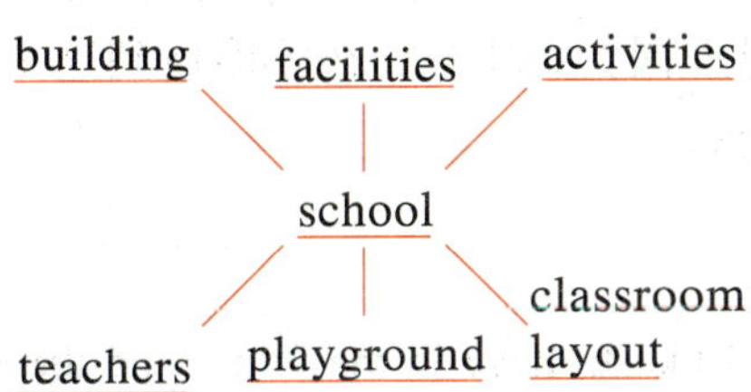

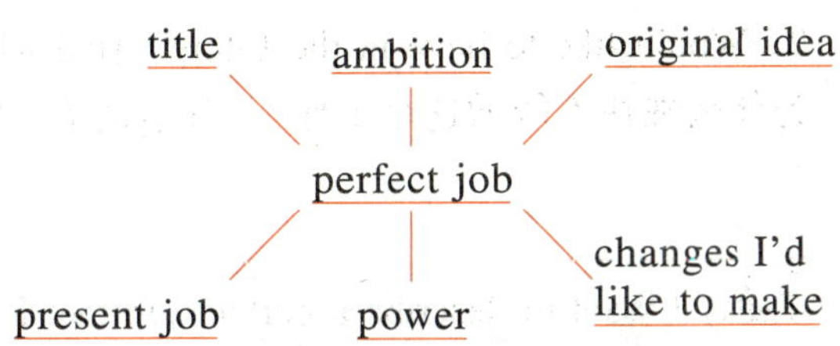

◇ Write down some words or phrases that you can think of to describe the topic given in the center. 脑洞大开，关于以下中心关键词，你能想到从哪些方面描述它，写下来吧。

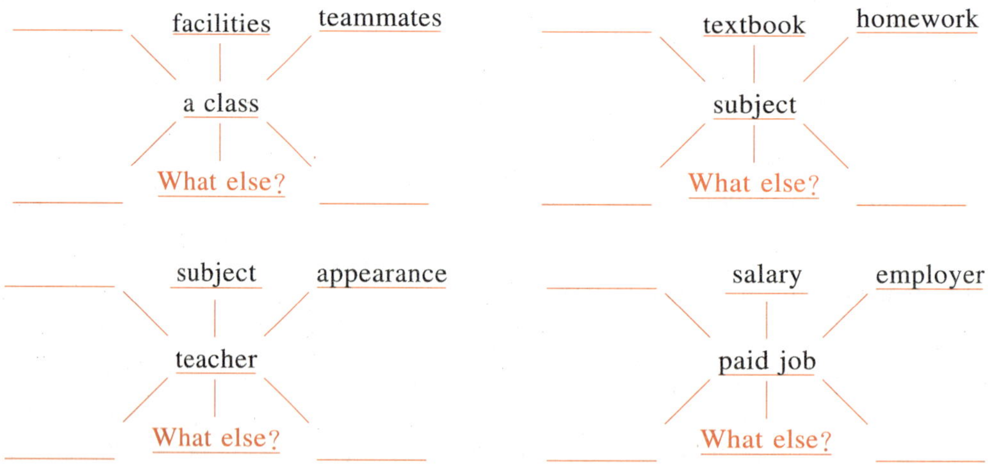

Module 2　实战演练

Describe a perfect job that you would like to have in the future
You should say:
What the job would be
What you would do in that job
How you can get the job
And explain why you would like to do that job

题目思路和方向

这是一个两层含义的问题(2-tier question)所以必须找出这个 part 2 问题的**两个关键词组**才能满足考官对考生答案的要求。一起通过一些问题和有用的理念来热热身吧：

1. Perfect job: Perfect 什么意思？你会选择怎么工作？为什么选择这个工作？工作期间会遇到什么？什么才算 perfect job？

a) A professor at college — flexible academic pace and fruitful research work.

b) A manager in a big firm — develop a career and realize one's self worth.

c) A skillful doctor — help to relieve people from suffering and live a fulfilling life.

d) Successful businessmen — have a sense of success and be able to help people in need.

2. Would like to have in the future: 什么时候想上岗？要准备什么才能做到这个工作？为什么现在不能做这个工作？(注意时态：将来式)

6 分答案

Today I want to describe a perfect job that I would like to have in the future and the job

I want to do is to become a skillful doctor. I guess the main reason for why I want to become a doctor is that I can help to relieve people from suffering and live a fulfilling life. I plan to fulfill this dream when I graduate from medical school which would take five to seven years. And if I work hard, I might become a senior doctor in ten years.

First of all, junior doctors work as general doctors when they start their careers in the hospital. However, junior doctors won't be able to work in nice hospitals as those are for really good doctors. I will either work in a hospital that my medical school is partnered with or have to work in a low level hospital that's usually very small and lack good equipment. Finally, because I will only be a junior doctor when I first start, I will have to follow a senior doctor and walk around the whole hospital to look at different patients with different medical problems. This means I will have to work long hours, maybe nine A. M. to nine P. M. , if I want to do my job well.

Although becoming a good doctor is very stressful and tiring, I think it is very meaningful and that is why I think this will be the perfect job for me.

点评-为什么是 6 分?

Coherence(6 分)	Lexical Resource (6 分)	Grammar Range and Structure (7 分)
✓ 使用一系列连接词。 × 但是无法保持回答连贯性(logical progression of ideas)。 × 回答偏短,未必能超过 part 2 回答要求(至少 1 分 30 秒)	✓ 有足够和针对性的词汇来回答问题但是有使用不当的地方。 ✓ 有展示明显的同义替换。 × 某些词汇多次重复。 × 展示少量"接地气"词汇但是同时也包含了写作应用词汇。	✓ 使用了简单和复杂句型来回答问题。 ✓ 大部分的句子和时态都正确。

高分词汇

skillful 熟练的
fulfilling life 充实的生活
fulfill 满足;应验;达成
work long hours 长时间工作
stressful 有压力的
meaningful 有意义的

高分答案

Right, I like to start the ball rolling by talking about an ideal job I'd like to have in the not too distant future and if I have the chance, I'd want to become a principle of a prestigious school or commander-in-chief of a successful training centre. I guess the biggest reason why I want to become a head-master or in some countries, the head-teacher, is that I'm really passionate about teaching and passing on my expertise to the next generation. Besides, I don't just want to educate students; I wanna train the best teachers possible and create an amazing learning environment for everyone.

So, you might be wondering how I set my sights on this crazy idea in the first place. I think it all originated when I was first became a teacher a couple of years ago. Yes, I was teaching amazing students. Yes, I was enjoying my job but after a couple of months, I was really frustrated with the working conditions. I was basically a workaholic day in, day out as I had to work late into the night to finish off marking copious amounts of homework. I was working unsociable hours which meant I couldn't hang out with my friends and spend time with my family. I felt so negative that I actually spoke to the principle directly about it, but guess what? He just swept me under the rug and told me to suck it up coz he said it's part of being a teacher.

If I'm lucky enough to fulfill my dream of becoming a principle, I will definitely restrain from saying things like that to my teachers as it really damages their ego. Furthermore, as their head-teacher, I'll organize proper training programmes and offer generous incentive schemes so that my teachers will feel like if they work hard, they will be rewarded. Finally, because of the power accompanied with the role of the head master, I can actually sculpt and manage every teacher's career path so that they can become great teachers in the future.

点评–为什么高分?

Coherence(8 分)	Lexical Resource (8 分)	Grammar Range and Structure (8 分)
✓ 使用多种类型连接词而且使用正确。 ✓ 使用正确的引导性词汇;整体答案有一定的连贯性。 ✓ 回答能达到 2 分钟的 part 2 最高要求。	✓ 自然灵活地使用适用不同词汇表达不同的意思。 ✓ 展示大量不常见词汇和习语。 ✓ 回答出现多种口语化词汇,脱离写作式回答。 ✓ 多次出现同义替换。	✓ 灵活运用多种复杂句型来回答问题。 ✓ 回答出现多种时态。 ✓ 没有明显的语法和时态错误。

高分词汇

prestigious 受尊敬的;有声望的
be wondering 觉得奇怪;疑惑的
frustrated 挫败的;失意
workaholic 工作狂
day in, day out 每天每夜
late into the night 直到深夜
copious amounts 大量的
unsociable hours 非正常工作时间(不是早九晚五)
swept me under the rug 不搭理
suck it up 强制接受
restrain 克制
ego 自尊心
proper training programmes 正式的培训项目

generous incentive schemes 丰富/有吸引力的奖金计划

rewarded 奖赏;奖励

sculpt and manage 创造并把控

> Describe a school you have attended in your childhood.
> You should say:
> Where it was
> What the classrooms were like
> What the teachers were like
> How you felt about this school

题目思路和方向(idea brainstorm)

这是一个两层问题(2-tier question),所以必须找出这个 part 2 问题的**三个关键词组**才能满足考官对考生答案的要求。一起通过一些问题和有用的理念来热热身吧:

1. A school:你会选哪个学校?为什么选这个学校?学校建筑/环境怎么样?对这个学校感觉如何?(注意:要和其他关键词配合)

a) Kindergarten — nursery school; playgroup; babysitter; pre-school

b) Primary school — grade school; grammar school; graded school; prep school

2. Attended:在学校上了什么课?和什么人一起上课?有没有什么开心/不开心的经历?

3. Childhood:小时后的什么时间段?小时后的事情你记得清楚吗?小时候对学校看法和现在对学校的看法有没有改变?

6 分答案

Today I want to describe a school I attended in my childhood and the school is called Shunde primary school. Shunde primary school is located in the middle of the city center within Huangpu district, which is mainly famous for its up-market shopping. Because the school is located in the heart of the city center, the school is very small. What I mean is, there are only two buildings which are white and brown and each building has three floors with five classrooms on each floor. I don't really like the colour because it's very dull and it looks like an old building. The school is also surrounded by silver metal fences and a large iron gate at the front for security reasons.

The biggest attraction of the school is its academic success and the awards the students have won in the past. Over the last 30 years since the school started, many students achieved high grades in the state primary school exams which meant they can attend really good secondary schools.

If you go outside the school, you will find many different shops. However, most of these shops are aimed towards students and their parents so they are usually fast food shops, clothing stores, and stationary/book stores. I still remember eating noodles during my lunch break after a stressful morning of doing academic exercises.

点评–为什么是 6 分?

Coherence(6 分)	Lexical Resource (6 分)	Grammar Range and Structure (7 分)
✓ 有引导词,每个段落都清楚明了。 × 但是回答缺乏连贯性,思维跳跃。 × 单句为主;没有充分运用不同的连接词。	✓ 灵活运用不同的词汇来回答问题。 × 但是限于一些常用词汇。 ✓ 展示多种形容词和词组。 × 但是欠缺更高级的同义替换形容词。 ✓ 出现了 1—2 次明显同义替换。	✓ 使用了简单和复杂句型来回答问题。 ✓ 能灵活运用多种语法结构来表达准确意思。 ✓ 回答里时态运用正确。 × 但是出现混乱不连贯的情况。

高分词汇

up-market shopping 奢侈品购物;高档产品购物
heart of the city center 市中心的核心地段
security reasons 安全理由
biggest attraction 最大的吸引点
state primary school exams 国家小学测试;国家小学考试
academic exercises 课堂练习

高分答案

Sure, I'm going to talk about the only school I went to when I was young and this school is called Chapmen primary school. I was pretty much living and breathing in the same area for the first ten years of my life so I guess it's the only education establishment I can speak about. I started attending this primary school when I was around five or six years old. I don't quite remember as it was quite some time ago. However, I still remember the how it looked like so I'll focus on that.

Chapmen primary school is one of the five international primary schools under the British school's foundation umbrella. What this means is that these primary schools are designed to emulate real top class schools in the U. K. in terms of building design, classroom layout, and educational facilities and I can say, Chapmen primary school is no exception. The school originally had four floors and two wings, east and west, but by the time I graduated, they had added another floor to accommodate the huge influx of students. Each floor basically represented different year groups. The ground floor classrooms belonged to year ones and twos, the first floor belonged to year threes and fours and so on. And at the end of each floor, you'd find a pretty decent library with computers and such for research, a music room with tons of instruments around the world, and the art's and craft's room where I spent lots of time making pottery and painting hideous pictures.

However, I guess the most memorable feature of the school is definitely its huge playground and the wonderful teachers that taught me throughout the six years when I was there. I spent so many lunchtime playing cops and robbers in the asphalt playground as well as playing down-ball in the down-ball courts which was right next to a miniature garden.

So yea, this is pretty much what I remember about the only school that I attended in my childhood.

点评–为什么高分?

Coherence(8 分)	Lexical Resource (8 分)	Grammar Range and Structure (8 分)
✓ 能充分展开而且对一两个描述点有足够的扩展。 ✓ 能灵活和准确使用多元化的连接词和信号词。 ✓ 回答能达到2 分钟的 part 2 最高要求。	✓ 适用多种中高级动词和形容词来准确描述话题。 ✓ 展示大量"接地气"的地道表达。 ✓ 回答看不出有写作的痕迹,完全是口语化的回答。 ✓ 多次出现同义替换。	✓ 灵活运用多种复杂句型来回答问题。 ✓ 回答里的时态统一,没有时态跳跃的情况。 ✓ 没有明显的语法和时态错误,准确度极高。

高分词汇

education establishment 学术机构
quite some time ago 一段时间前
I'll focus on 我会集中在
emulate 模仿
top-class 顶尖;一流水平
no exception 无一例外
accommodate 容纳
huge influx 大量进入的;大量流入的
belonged to 属于
decent 合宜的;相当好的
tons of 非常多
hideous 丑恶;丑陋
memorable feature 难忘的事情;难忘的细节
asphalt 沥青,柏油

Module 3 Speech 的结构

一个好的演讲一定是一气呵成、逻辑清晰的,下面总结的一些结构语句,考生平时可以多加练习,在自己的话题卡描述中清晰地展开出开头 beginning,强调 key point 以及结尾等。

开头 I'm going to talk about/I'd like to talk about/Let me tell you about + 话题

强调 I guess the most memorable feature of the school is/What's remarkable is that + 要强调的内容

结尾　So, yea, this is pretty much what I remember about + 话题

Module 4　练习

TIPS:

考试中,考官会给考生一分钟的时间 take notes 记笔记。这一分钟的时间非常宝贵,要好好把握。笔记字数尽量少,只要自己看得懂就可以了。在高分答案的笔记中,"5 - 6"表示"5 - 6 years old",没有必要写全。

尽量用缩写。

1) 同学们可以自创一些缩写。例如 T 就是作者自创的缩写,表示 Teachers。

2) 在 Study 这个话题中,经常会提到 Teachers 和 Students,建议大家做笔记时,用"T"代表"Teachers",用"Ss"代表"Students"。

3) 写中文也是可以的。

◇ Now write your notes within 1 min and then give a speech about it. 计时练习!一分钟时间记笔记,两分钟时间陈述。

Practice 1

Describe a project (or homework) you did as part of your studies.
You should say:
what the project or work was
when you did this
who was with you
how easy or difficult it was
and explain how you felt afterwards

Notes:

Practice 2

Describe something interesting you learnt from the internet.
You should say:
what you learnt
what website you learnt it from
how you learnt it
and explain why you think it was interesting.

Notes:

Practice 3

Describe a person whose job is useful to the society.
You should say:
who the person is
where the person works
what the person does
and explain why you think this person's job is important.

Notes:

Practice 4

> Describe a small company in your hometown that you think is successful.
> You should say:
> what the company is
> what this company produces
> how you knew about this company
> and explain why you think this company is successful.

Notes:

Part 3 Discussion

Module 1 考题回顾

Part 2 结束后，考官会根据 Part 2 考生的回答，更加深入地问一些问题，所谓深入，也就是说这些问题会更加思辨以及具有一定的社会话题性。以下是学习与工作话题中，考官常问的一些问题。

1. Do you think learning about history has any benefits for children?
2. What kinds of people become school teachers?
3. Why do young people keep changing jobs?
4. What kinds of work skills are important in China?
5. In order to reach an equality of education, do you think it's a must for everyone to receive college education?

同学们会发现这些问题虽然形式与 Part 1 相同，考官提问考生回答，但是内容上比 Part 1 更为深刻，也就更有难度。在备考中，希望拿到高分的考生，可以多关注社会话题，在一些外文网站中找到灵感，也让你的答案内容更有思想，不会空洞贫乏。例如，第 6 题主要讨论了教育平等以及大学教育的问题，我们在备考中可以在外文网站输入关键词，搜索出一些相应的报道或评论。这些内容都会给我们的答案加分。

网站推荐：

www. educationnext. org

www. aol. com

◇ Read about Shanna Walton's opinion on *equality of educational opportunity* and write your own thoughts about this topic. 阅读下文中 Shanna Walton 的观点，并写出你的观点。

http://www.bcdef.com/ Education

Equality of Educational Opportunity

comment on this topic

Shanna Walton says:
04/09/2016 at 1:10 pm

All students are not equal and never will be. Over the past 55 years every program tried to close the achievement gap has failed. Let' s focus on helping each student be the best they can to their level. Pushing all to college prep is wrong and results in thousands of drop outs, which does nothing to fill the thousands of good jobs that go begging and don't require college degrees.

Submit

Module 2 Debate & Discussion

Debate: Work in two teams and debate. You have two minutes to think about what you are going to say. 分2组，围绕以下话题，进行辩论。(准备时间：2分钟)

Which do you think is better, students studying in big classes or studying in small classes?

Team A

Opinion 1 ______________________

Opinion 2 ______________________

Opinion 3 ______________________

Team B

Opinion 1 ______________________

Opinion 2 ______________________

Opinion 3 ______________________

Discussion: Discuss and answer the question below. 讨论以下话题。

Why do some young people prefer to be unemployed?

Part 4 Language Use

Module 1 语法改错

1. My sister is a workaholic. He often works overtime.
2. She love cats.
3. My grandfather is a fireman. He has retired since last year.
4. We talked about if universities should charge tuition fees.
5. There are three main reasons of this change.

Module 2 语音练习

Direction: match words with correspondent phonetic according to the underline alphabet. 根据划线的字母将单词填入相对应的音标方框中。

keep; lip; study; life; white; live; walk; work; laugh; assignment; contribute; assist; diligent; discipline; active; math; biology; attention; mean

[iː]	[i]	[ə]

续表

[ai]	[æ]	[ɔ]

Chapter 3 Family & Relationships

话题词汇热身训练

Module 1 词汇

◇ Exercise 1. Make the following into sentences and read the sentences aloud. 用下列单词组成句子并大声朗读。

n.	*v.*	*adj.*
empathy	comfort	casual
security	chat	close
guidance	blame	influential
nuclear family	adore	supportive
cousin	get on well with	caring
willpower	hold on to	good-looking
dimple	long for	considerate
generation gap	look after	mature
role model	chill out	slim
bestie	raise	muscular
bosom friend	socialize	stubborn
the elder	respect	down-to-earth
emergency	share sth. in common	intelligent
sense of humor	explore	positive
parenting	overcome	rude
pal	be of medium height	mean
homesickness	represent	talkative
	mingle around	plain
	keep in contact	awkward

1. I/used to/live/granny/childhood.

Example: I used to live with my granny in my childhood.

2. I/remember/day/we first/met/library.

3. Moody/affect/others/around you/colleagues/friends.

4. Friendship/mean/a lot/me/I/believe/it/lays/foundation/many/our relationships.

5. Mark Zuckerburg/who/made/efforts/education/role model/young.

◇ Exercise 2. Write down some words or phrases that you can think of within 30 seconds to answer these questions. And then work in pairs to ask and answer these questions. 流利度达成——30 秒内写出你能想到的可以回答下列问题的单词或词组！并与你身边的同学两人一组互相提问回答这些问题。

1. When do you spend time with your family?

2. Do you often go out with your friends?

3. Do you have many relatives?

4. Do you like to receive gifts?

5. Would you like to hang out with strangers?

直击考点

Module 1 Connectives 连接词

Give examples

Underline the connectives in the sentences and replace them with the following phrases. 下划线划出每句中代表“举例子”的连接词，并用方框内补充的词组连接词替换写句子。

for instance	like	and things like that
in some cases . . .	take myself as an example	

1. He taught us not only a subject, but also how to carry on learning about the subject after class. For example, he said that we should always try to keep an enquiring and open mind.

2. You can't tell many things just from the appearance, such as the past, hobbies, eating habits and so on.

3. The Internet provides people with entertainment, such as watching movie, chatting room and even shopping.

4. Steve is a huge fan of online shopping while I'm not that into it, like I could only do online shopping once a month.

5. Sometimes staying with friends is more relaxing than staying with family.

Module 2 Paraphrase 词群同义转换

◇ Write down the synonyms of the following words and describe the word to your group members. 写出下列单词的同义词，并用自己话向身边的同学描述这个单词。

Example：responsibility：obligation，duty，liability

✓ something not easy and may require a lot of efforts

like（喜欢）：

enjoyment：pastime，recreation，entertainment

outgoing：energetic，active，open-hearted，

People who provide you with guidance and help in academic studies

kind（友善的）：nice，understanding，sweet，lovely，gentle

Part 1 Interview

Module 1 Do you prefer ... 个人偏好

Do you prefer A or B？这样的个人偏好的题型在雅思口语的 Part 1 中并不是难题，但

是考生需要注意首先听好考官问的两个选项，不要听错，注意集中注意力。其次，虽然这类的考题大家在答题思路上不会出现没话说的现象，但是答案中的语法却会出现不准确的情况。下面，我们来学习个人偏好的疑问句该如何回答。

1. prefer + *n.* /V-ing + to/rather than + *n.* /V-ing.

I prefer non-fiction to fiction.

I prefer the latter picture to the former.

I prefer traveling by day rather than by night.

I prefer jogging than swimming.

2. prefer + to do + rather than + do.

I prefer to read a book rather than watch TV.

◇ Some of the following sentences are incorrect. Find those incorrect ones among all of them and rewrite it based on the grammar rules you learned. 句子改错！找出下列句子中有错误的句子，并重新改写。

1. They prefer to go with us rather than to stay at home.

______________________________.

2. I prefer hanging out with outgoing people to introverted.

______________________________.

3. He prefers to climbing to take the lesson.

______________________________.

4. I prefer to stand on my own two feet rather than turned to my parents.

______________________________.

5. Compared with going out for dinner alone, I always prefer to go with my pals.

______________________________.

◇ Exercise. Answer the following questions. 回答下列问题。

1. Do you prefer to spend time with your family or with your friends?

2. Do you prefer to be alone or to be with friends?

3. Do you want to hang out with a group of people or with a few friends?

Module 2 实战演练

➢ Examiner: What gifts did you receive in your childhood?

Well I could hardly remember anything to be honest, coz it's kind of far from my recent life. As I remember I had something like a toy car, and toy highways. Yeah, it's like you can build up a city on your own. And there are different types of vehicles like sedans, coaches and even police cars. It's really cool.

➢ Examiner: How do people in your country celebrate birthdays?

Normally people would have a big meal with family or friends. Some young people might prefer to have a party and stuff, though I haven't got any birthday parties for ages. For the past few years I was either not here in China or preparing for tests and exams or things like that.

➢ Examiner: Do you think family members should live together? (Why? /Why not?)

Frankly I prefer to live alone. It doesn't mean that I don't like being together with my family. Actually I treat my family as a very important part of life. I just feel more comfortable to live by myself. You know everyone gets a caring but sometimes over concerned mom.

➢ Examiner: When you were a child, which of your relatives did you spend the most time with?

My granny. My granny took care of me during my childhood. She cooked dinner for me and taught me everything in life. She's a kind and lovely old lady. She's really passionate and warm-hearted. Everyone enjoys talking with her since she always smiles to others.

➢ Examiner: What does friendship mean to you?

Friendship means companionship. Friendship gives me strength and courage. Honestly I always feel lucky when I think of the bunch of friends around me. They are enthusiastic and most importantly they will always be there whenever I'm happy or sad. Like my favorite character Pheobe in the classic American TV series "friends" once said: boyfriend comes and goes but friendship lasts forever. I really like that.

➢ Examiner: What do you usually do with your friends?

A lot of things, like travelling, having dinner, watching movies and chatting in a café, coz I always feel relaxed staying with my friends. And friends are normally people who share similar hobbies with you. So sometimes we do sports together too, for instance jogging and squash.

Discourse Markers

上一章我们讲到了话语标记 Discourse Markers 的作用。大家在使用 Discourse Markers 时，也要注意 Discourse Markers 和所说的内容的一致。

例题：Do you do any housework?

Student A：To be honest, I do a lot of housework such as mopping the floor and washing the dishes.

Student B：Well, I do a lot of housework such as mopping the floor and washing the dishes.

Student C：I'd have to say that housework is something that I do all the time such as mopping the floor and washing the dishes.

答案分析：

同学A,B和C都满足问题的要求,成功回答问题。但是,如果大家细心看看原题,大家会发现三位同学用的话语标记都用的不对。

A同学："To be honest" 或者"To be frank"都是中国学生喜欢用的开场白。但是,你们要知道这两句的真正意义是告诉考官你的答案和想象中很不一样。正确的用法应该是这样：

To be honest, I've never done any housework in my life since my helper does it for me all the time。

B同学："well" 可以说是中国学生最受欢迎的话语标记。其实,"well" 的真正意思是"我了解你的问题但是我需要点时间想想"。如果大家需要回答那么简单的问题时(Do you do any housework?),开始回答时用 "well"是不合适的,因为这个是一个黑/白问题。学生只需要回答有做+example或者没做就行。

错误的用 "well" 会让考官觉得你不诚恳,随时会让你的流利度分数下降到5分以下。如果学生真的要用 "well",就必需展示深度想法的表达：

Well, it depends ....

Well, sort of ....

Well, not really. You see ...

Well, I'm not sure exactly ....

Module 3　练习

1. What kind of gifts do you like to receive?

2. How did you celebrate your birthdays when you were a child?

3. Do you still feel that celebrating your birthday is important?

4. What do you do on your birthday now?

5. Do you live with your family?

6. In the future, do you think you will have more opportunities to see your relatives?

7. Who do you feel is the most important member of your family?

8. Do you have a lot of friends?

9. How often do you hang out with your friends?

10. What do you usually do when you hang out with your friends?

11. Do you prefer to share your ideas with your friends or parents?

12. Do you think it's important for friends to meet regularly?

13. Do you prefer to live with your parents or alone?

14. Are you good at making friends with new people?

Part 2 The Long-turn

Module 1 Brainstorming 头脑风暴

◇ Read the examples of a brainstorming exercise. 请看以下头脑风暴的例子。

- mum
  - job
    - (now) housewife
      - preparing meals
      - doing housework
    - (used to be) model
  - appearance
    - stunning
    - slim
  - personality
    - outgoing
    - positive
  - why I spend most time with her
    - want to be as beautiful as her
    - she comforts me
    - we do things together

I barely knew Mr Wong.

↓

Mr. Wong asked for my help.

↓

Mr Wong's dog ran away.

↓

I helped Mr. Wong to find his dog.

↓

We found Mr. Wong's dog.

↓

Mr. Wong and I became friends.

◇ Write down some words or phrases that you can think of to describe the topic given in the center. 脑洞大开，关于以下中心关键词，你能想到从哪些方面描述它，写下来吧。

- interesting old person
  - hobbies
    - horse-riding
    - ______
  - ______
    - ______
    - ______
  - ______
    - ______
    - ______
  - ______
    - ______
    - ______

- intelligent person
  - study
    - high scores
    - ______
  - ______
    - ______
    - ______
  - ______
    - ______
    - ______
  - ______
    - ______
    - ______

a success my friend has had

↓

At first, . . .

↓

______

↓

______

↓

______

↓

Finally, he succeed.

Module 2 实战演练

> Describe a family member who you spend the most time with.
> You should say:
> who the person is
> when you usually are together
> what kind of person he or she is
> what you usually do (when you are) together
> and explain why you spend more time with this person than with other members of your family.

题目思路和方向(idea brainstorm)

这是一个两层问题(2-tier question)所以必须找出这个 part 2 问题的**两个关键词组**才能满足考官对考生答案的要求。一起通过一些问题和有用的理念来热热身吧：

1. Family member：这位家人是谁？可以形容一下他/她吗？和他/她关系怎么样？

a) Immediate family members — Mum, Dad, Brother, Sister.

b) Close family members — Grandparents, Uncle, Auntie.

c) Related family members — Cousins.

2. You spend the most time with：为什么和他/她相处最长时间？和他/她相处的时候干吗？和他/她相处的时候有什么感受？以后想继续和他/她相处吗？

6 分答案

Today I want to describe a family member who I spend the most time with and this person is my uncle. My uncle's called Bob and he grew up in a small city in the center of the Guangdong province but now resides in Shanghai. That's why whenever he speaks mandarin to me, he has a little bit of a Cantonese accent which sounds a little weird. I see him very often because I'm currently studying in a boarding school in the U. K. and he always comes to U. K. for business trips. Every time he comes to the U. K. he would come visit me at the boarding school which makes me feel very warm and loved.

He's in his late 40 s as he has greying hair as far as I can recall. Although he is quite old now, he's quite a handsome man with a chiseled face and high cheekbones. Sadly, he's not married at the moment so I think that's why he treats me so well. Besides this, my uncle has a very good personality. He is always smart and outgoing and that's why I always feel positive when I see him. Furthermore, because of his personality, he is a very successful businessman. In fact, he owns ten companies in the U. K. so he has to fly between China and the U. K. all the time. This is all I have to say and this is why my uncle is the family member I spend the most time with.

为什么是 6 分?

Coherence(6 分)	Lexical Resource (6 分)	Grammar Range and Structure (7 分)
× 信号词欠缺;可能导致结构混乱。 × 没有出现话语标记;考生可能出现明显的停顿。 × 回答偏短,未必能超过 part 2 回答要求(至少 1 分 30 秒)。	✓ 有足够的形容词来描述主题; × 但是可以更深入地去展开内容。 ✓ 展示少量"接地气"词汇; × 但是同时也包含了写作应用词汇。 ✓ 有展示明显的同义替换。	✓ 使用了简单和复杂句型来回答问题。 ✓ 大部分的句子和时态都正确。

高分词汇

Resides 住在

warm and loved 感觉温暖和被爱着的

chiseled face 轮廓分明的脸

high cheekbones 位置高的颧骨

outgoing 开朗

feel positive 感觉正面的

高分答案

Okay, allow me to tell you about a family member who I spend the most time with and this person would definitely be my mum, Frances. Before I talk about why I love to spend time with her, I'd like to describe her a little. So, first things first, because my mum's a housewife, she spends a lot of time at home. Her main duties include preparing meals for me and my dad as well as doing the house work after my Dad leaves for work and I leave for school.

Although she's a housewife now, my mum used to be a catwalk model before she got married to my dad. What I'm trying to say here is even though my mum is now a stay-at-home wife, she still looks absolutely stunning. She'd make sure she exercises on her cross-fit trainer for thirty minutes a day in order to maintain her slim figure. Besides this, because she's really concerned with her beauty, she'd make sure she applies a facial mask every night before she goes to bed so she'll always look her best when we see her in the morning.

Now, as for why I like to spend time with her, let me see ... I think the biggest reason isn't just because I want look as beautiful as her, but because of her personality. She's really outgoing and positive all the time. Every time I have a bad day at school, the first thing I do once the school bell rings is to run back home, jump into her arms, and get her to give me a big hug as well as comfort me at the same time. Furthermore, when I have day off school, no matter what I do, I'll always spend it with my mum coz she'll always think of something interesting and creative to do. I'm never bored when I'm around her so that's why I spend the most time with her.

点评-为什么高分？

Coherence（8 分）	Lexical Resource（7 分）	Grammar Range and Structure（8 分）
✓ 能充分展开而且对一两个描述点有足够的扩展（特别是人物的背景）。 ✓ 能灵活和准确使用多元化的连接词和信号词。 ✓ 回答能达到 2 分钟的 part 2 最高要求。	✓ 使用了中高级词汇； × 但是可以适当地增加比较地道的习语和俚语。 × 在第二个段落有点像写作的回答而不是口语的回答。 ✓ 多次出现同义替换。	✓ 灵活运用过去、现在时态来全面描述话题里的人物。 ✓ 多次使用复杂结构来准确展开话题和保持连贯性。 ✓ 没有明显的语法和时态错误，准确度极高。

高分词汇

main duties 主要的任务；主要做的事儿
stay-at-home wife 家庭主妇
absolutely stunning 非常漂亮/帅气；毋庸置疑的漂亮/帅气
maintain 保持
slim figure 苗条的身材
concerned 顾虑
look her best 保持最佳状态
positive 正面的
jump into her arms 进她怀抱里
I'm around her 和她一起的时候

> Describe a neighbor that you helped
> You should say:
> who this person is
> when you helped this person
> and explain why you helped this person.

题目思路和方向（idea brainstorm）

这是一个两层问题（2-tier question），所以必须找出这个 Part 2 问题的**两个关键词组**才能满足考官对考生答案的要求。一起通过一些问题和有用的理念来热热身吧：

1. A Neighbor：这位邻居是谁？可以描述他/她？怎么认识他/她？多久见一次？

a）Background — 住在哪里？什么职业？

b）Appearance — 多大？身高？长相？

c）Personality — 个性？对他/她个性的评价？

d）Lifestyle — 生活习惯？为什么有这些生活习惯？

e）What you like/dislike about him/her — 你喜欢他/她什么？为什么？

2. You helped：为什么要帮他/她？帮他/她之前你在干什么？帮他/她的时候发生什么事？帮他/她之后有没有感谢你？

6 分答案

Today I want to describe a neighbor that I helped and this neighbor is called Mrs. Chan. I met Mrs. Chan for the time when I was moving into my new house around 5 years ago. She lives in a house just down the street so I can say we are close neighbors. I had a lot of boxes to carry and I was all by myself at the time. Mrs. Chan was very kind and offered to help me carry the heavy boxes into my house.

Moving onto how often I see her, I actually see her quite often. I'd always see her watering her garden or planting something in the patio. When I run past her house I'd always say hi to her and she'd greet me with a big smile. I rarely have the opportunity to talk to her because she looks like she's always busy. As for what sort of person she is, Mrs. Chan is a middle-aged woman with curly black hair and has two big eyes and a small nose. She's not very tall and she looks a bit plump when I spoke with her last time. Mrs. Chan is a very kind and polite person as I said before.

Finally, I'd explain why I helped Mrs. Chan. I still remember after I moved most of my boxes into the house, I heard Mrs. Chan scream. When I ran out to see what happened, I saw Mrs. Chan and my boxes on the floor. She had hurt her back when she was helping me carry the boxes and she was crying because she was in pain. I helped her get up and took her back to her house. And because she hurt her back and could not do her shopping for the day, I helped her do her daily shopping at the local supermarket and brought all the shopping back to her house so she didn't need to leave the house.

为什么是 6 分?

Coherence(6 分)	Lexical Resource (7 分)	Grammar Range and Structure (6 分)
✓ 善用话语标记。 × 但是可能出现过于逻辑的表达,不是真正的口语表达。 ✓ 使用了连词。 × 但只使用了简单和少量的连词(because, and)。	✓ 有使用大量形容词。 × 但是都是偏简单。 ✓ 展示"接地气"词汇和不常用词汇。 × 但是同时也包含了写作应用词汇。 ✓ 有展示明显的同义替换。	✓ 使用了简单和复杂句。 × 但是大部分都是简单句。 ✓ 大部分的句子和时态都正确。

高分词汇

just down the street 同一条街
offered to help 愿意提供协助
greet 打招呼
big smile 灿烂的笑容
curly black hair 卷卷的黑头发
plump 体型偏胖

高分答案

Hmmmm, it's really hard to choose as I've helped so many neighbors in the past but I guess the first person that popped into my head is Mr. Wong. Now, why Mr. Wong then? I still remember it was a thundery summer evening. I was too tired to cook my own dinner after a long day at work so I decided to get some takeaway and whilst I was waiting for the delivery, I heard a loud knock at the door. I thought it was my food arriving but I was pretty shocked when I saw it was Mr. Wong standing in the doorway. You see, I was surprised coz we rarely spoke to each other and the only time we saw each other was when we were waiting for the lift to arrive. And to be frank, I didn't know much about him back then. All I knew was he lived in the flat just across mine and he works as a fitness trainer so he's pretty well built and he towers over me in terms of height.

Anyhow, after the initial shock of seeing Mr. Wong on my doorstep, I started to realize something was wrong. His jet black hair was all wet and soggy and I could see two streams of tears rolling down his face. He looked very panicky, which is very different to how he normally acts. He's usually very calm and collected and every time I see him, he's the happy go lucky guy. I quickly asked what was wrong, and he told me that he forgot to close his door and his dog ran away. He tried knocking on other neighbors' doors but none of them responded. So, seeing how helpless he was, I quickly grabbed my keys and followed him out so we could find his dog together.

At first I thought his dog might have ran down the stairs onto the streets, but after noticing how bad the weather was outside, I thought maybe his dog didn't leave the building at all. That's why I decided to check the staircases first and luckily enough, his dog was hiding behind one of the dustbins on one of the floors. I quickly shouted for Mr. Wong to come and a few seconds later, he appeared, looking all relived. After this incident, Mr. Wong and I became great friends and I still keep in contact with him even though I've now moved to a new accommodation.

点评–为什么高分?

Coherence(7 分)	Lexical Resource (8 分)	Grammar Range and Structure (8 分)
× 故事背景描述有点偏多,有离题的嫌疑。 ✓ 能灵活和准确使用多元化的连接词和信号词。 ✓ 回答能达到 2 分钟的 part 2 最高要求。	✓ 使用多种中高级动词和形容词来准确描述话题。 ✓ 展示大量"接地气"的地道表达。 ✓ 回答看不出有写作的痕迹,完全是口语化的回答。 ✓ 多次出现同义替换。	✓ 灵活运用过去、现在时态来全面描述话题里的人物。 ✓ 多次使用复杂结构来准确展开话题和保持连贯性。 ✓ 没有明显的语法和时态错误,准确度极高。

高分词汇

thundery summers evening 夏天打雷的天气
loud knock 大声敲门
shocked 被吓倒
rarely spoke 不常说话
just across mine 在我的……对面
well built 身体很“壮”
towers over me 比我高很多
wet and soggy 湿透的
calm and collected 冷静和镇定的
happy go lucky guy 乐观的人
helpless 无助

Module 3　Speech 的结构

在描述事件类的演讲中，要使逻辑清晰，可以使用一下结构语句，清晰地展现出事件发展的过程。一般来说，一件事情的发展可以被分为开始、进展和结果几个阶段。

开头　First of all, I realized that + 事件开头
进展　Then/After .../Before ...　+ 事件的发展
结尾　Finally/Eventually + 事件的结果

Module 4　练习

TIPS：

上一章我们提到，在考试中考官会给考生一分钟的时间 take notes 记笔记，然后再让考生开始演讲。记笔记的作用是：如果考生在演讲的过程中突然没了思路，就可以扫一眼笔记，所以笔记应当清晰明了、重点突出。

要注意的是，考生在记笔记时写下关键词即可，避免写长句子。一是因为 1 分钟的时间是来不及写句子的，二是因为考生在演讲时只能扫一眼笔记，而不能停下来去阅读笔记，如果记笔记时句子写得又长又复杂，考生回过头来看的时候可能来不及看完整个句子。

以下是一个基本无效的笔记：

Let me tell you about my uncle. He plays a very important role in my life. He is a very considerate and thoughtful person who has always done her best to help me make decisions in the face of day-to-day difficulties ....

以下是一个有效的笔记：

uncle
personality: helps me: homework
responsibleteaches me: writing
determinedencourages me: be independent
curiousgives advice:

◇ Now write your notes within 1 min and then give a speech about it. 计时练习！一分钟时间记笔记，两分钟时间陈述。

Practice 1

Describe a friend who you had at school.
You should say:
what he/she looked like
where you first met
how you became friends
what you did together
and explain why you remember him/her so well.

Notes:

Practice 2

Describe a person you know who is beautiful or handsome.
You should say:
who the person is
when you met the person at the first time
what the person's character is
and explain how you feel about the person.

Notes:

Practice 3

Describe a happy family event from your childhood that you remember well.
You should say:
what the event was
when and where it happened
what you saw or did
and explain why you remember this even so well.

Notes:

Practice 4

Describe a time that you and your friend had a disagreement.
You should say
when this happened
who you disagreed with
what you and your friend argued about
and explain if you solved the disagreement.

Notes:

Part 3 Discussion

Module 1 考题回顾

本章的话题 Family & Relationships 相对来说是比较简单的，因为 Family & Relationships 是与我们的生活息息相关的，是我们每一个人都可以有话可说的话题。以下是 Part 3 部分，Family & Relationships 话题中，考官常问的一些问题。

1. How do people make friends?
2. Do you think it is easy for people to make friends at work?
3. Is it important for people to have good relationship with colleagues?
4. Have you ever helped a friend by giving advice?
5. What do you think of the whole family eating together?
6. Why do people need to sustain a constant relationship with their relatives and friends?

同学们会发现这些问题虽然形式与 Part 1 相同，考官提问考生回答，但是，内容上比 Part 1 更为深刻，也就更有难度。在备考中，希望拿到高分的考生，可以多关注 Family & Relationship 话题，在一些外文网站中找到灵感，也让你的答案内容更有思想，不会空洞贫乏。例如，第 1 题主要讨论人们如何交朋友，我们在备考中可以在外文网站输入关键词，搜索出一些相应的报道或评论。这些内容都会给我们的答案加分。

网站推荐：

www. economist. com

www. answer. com

◇ Read the tips on *making friends* and write your own thoughts about this topic. 阅读下文中关于如何交朋友的小贴士，并写出你的观点。

http://www.bcdef.com/ Education

Making and keeping friends can be particularly tough if you are shy or unsure of yourself. The best way to make new friends is to be involved in activities at school and in the community where there are other people your age.

Another way to make friends is to be friendly and helpful to other people. Talk to people, get to know them, and find out if you have something in common with them.

Module 2 Debate & Discussion

Debate: Work in two teams and debate. You have two minutes to think about what you are going to say. 分2组，围绕以下话题，进行辩论。(准备时间：2分钟)

Do you like to go out with a big group or just a few friends?

Team A	Team B
Opinion 1 ______	Opinion 1 ______
Opinion 2 ______	Opinion 2 ______
Opinion 3 ______	Opinion 3 ______

Discussion: Discuss and answer the question below. 讨论以下话题。

Is it easy to find real friends on social network?

Part 4 Language Use

Module 1 语法改错

1. I used to go swimming in the river when I live in the countryside.
2. You can download movies and store it in your computer.

3. Many articles on this topic are available through the internet.
4. People should act according to what they are believing.
5. There have an oak tree in my garden.

Module 2 语音练习

Direction: match words with correspondent phonetic according to the underline alphabet. 根据划线的字母将单词填入相对应的音标方框中。

think; there; they; this; sink; say; thought; very; where; various; university; white; wage; always

[θ]	[ð]	[s]
[v]	[w]	

Chapter 4 Hobbies & Sports

话题词汇热身训练

Module 1 词汇

◇ Exercise 1. Make the following into sentences and read the sentences aloud. 用下列单词组成句子并大声朗读。

n.	*v.*	*adj.*
sitting machine	relieve stress	athletic
rowing machine	keep fit	bony
workout	go cycling	strenuous
gym	sweat	regular
hiking	take a break	systematic
jogging	tone up my body	relaxing
yoga	lose weight	entertaining
a whole-body exercise	stretch	beneficial
breaststroke	get together with	individual
baseball	unwind	agreeable
sky-diving	go on a date	educational
novel	sing karaoke	indoor
badminton	capture	outdoor
racket	relax	recreational
sneakers	sacrifice	beneficial
push-up	devote	influential
involvement	have fun	
digital camera	spend	
pros and cons	cultivate	

1. I/try/hiking/as/often/possible.

I try to go hiking as often as possible.

2. As/high-school/student/there/not/much/I/do/change/my/daily routine

3. Ping-pong/no longer/popular/in China, and I remember/used to/play/all the time/when/I/kid.

4. City/colleges/educational attractions/museums and zoos.

5. Weekends/a great time/practice/healthy behaviors/you/have/more time/to do.

◇ Exercise 2. Write down some words or phrases that you can think of within 30 seconds to answer these questions. And then work in pairs to ask and answer these questions. 流利度达成——30 秒内写出你能想到的可以回答下列问题的单词或词组！并与你身边的同学两人一组互相提问回答这些问题。

1. What do people do on weekend?

2. Are you interested in sport?

3. Where do people in China usually exercise?

4. How do you relax?

5. Do you have a hobby?

直击考点

Module 1 Connectives 连接词

Contrast and Comparison

Fill in the gaps with words or phrases in the form. 用方框里相应的连接词或词组填空。

Words to show that things are similar	Words to show that things are different
Similarly	Whereas
Equally	On the other hand
Likewise	Instead of
As with	Alternatively
Like	Otherwise
In the same way	Unlike
Also	However
Both	But
	Although
	In contrast

1. Tom is always indifferent towards everything, ________, he doesn't want to depend upon others.

2. Ben wants to be a reporter. ________, he also thinks he would make a fine chef.

3. But at least some people find it ________ useful to have the negative pointed out and explained.

4. Most people do not seem to see family business ________ that they see other jobs.

5. ________, you can register online and enjoy hundreds of movies at home.

6. ________ doing outdoor sports he prefers painting and other indoor activities.

7. Penny suggested going hiking, ________, no one agreed on that.

Module 2 Paraphrase 词群同义转换

◇ Write down the synonyms of the following words and describe the word to your group members. 写出下列单词的同义词，并用自己话向身边的同学描述这个单词。

Example: schedule: plan, timetable, a to-do list, arrangement

✓ a plan that lists all the work that you have to do and when you must do each thing

healthy: ____

____

relax: ____

____

hobby: ____

____

popular: ____

____

Part 1 Interview

Module 1 Explain 解释说明

在雅思口语考试中，考官经常在 part 1 中追问，why？本书在第一章节的考试评分标准中也分析并且强调了雅思考试中考生想要考到理想的分数（6 分及以上），回答中一定要符合 willing to speak at length 的要求。因此大家在面对考官的追问时，通常是他认为你答的还不够充分，watch out！这个时候就不能再简单回答，一定要多做解释。

此外,考官也经常会问 What's the reason ....? 直接就某个话题的原因进行提问,例如:

What's the reason for the popularity of swimming?

What's the cause of gym's popularity?

How come jogging is so popular?

那么这个章节我们就来重点掌握在问答环节中作解释说明的方法。

1. 多种理由,重点强调

One of the reasons gym becomes more and more popular **is that** people realize that regular and systematic training is more effective than some simple workout.

Among all the factors, a pursuit of well-being **comes first.**

The increasing awareness of health care **plays a part in** people accepting more various types of sports in China.

其他理由补充:

While at the same time, a healthy diet is important too.

Another cause is that ....

2. 一个单一理由

The only reason that comes to my mind is convenience.

The root of the problem is people are sacrificing their time on commuting.

◇ Exercise. Answer the following questions. 回答下列问题。

1. Why do many people like swimming?

2. Why do some people do not like taking photographs?

Module 2　实战演练

➢ Examiner: Do you think people should get more money if they work on weekends?

No doubt. People usually work 8 hours per day in China. Well the situation might be different in other countries. But I guess everyone deserves an extra bonus or pay to make up for the weekends they sacrifice.

➢ Examiner: Do you like any particular sports?

Yep! I'm a huge fan of rock-climbing. I joined a rock-climbing club last year. At first I was scared and timid as a beginner and then I conquered the fear. It's a sport that strengthens your power and cultivates your sense of balance.

➤ Examiner: What are the advantages of doing regular exercise?

Well there are too many benefits of doing regular exercise. Exercise controls weight. Take myself as an example, I lost almost 15 pounds since last summer coz I kept jogging for like 20 minutes every morning. What's more, exercise improves mood. It brings you with a good mood. That's really important.

➤ Examiner: How do you usually relax (in your spare time)?

I normally go to watch a movie. That's my favorite way of relaxing, coz honestly attending parties and stuff brings me pressure as well. I guess I have the so called social activity phobia. I feel uncomfortable hanging out with unfamiliar people.

➤ Examiner: What are good hobbies, and what are bad hobbies?

In my perspective good hobbies improve your well-being either physically or mentally, such as reading, sports, or even painting. However, bad hobbies have negative effects on your life such as binge drinking and computer gaming. Well actually I'm not saying it's definitely bad to play games. It's in fact a matter of how long you spend on games.

➤ Examiner: Do you like to take photographs?

Sure! I love taking pictures. Moments happen all the time and they happen fast. Photography freezes them and so that we can enjoy them later. I have a digital camera and I use it to capture everything in my life, like my kitten pouncing on a ball of yarn and my bestie's birthday party.

Discourse Markers

在演讲时使用 discourse markers 能使你的意思更加明确，使考官更容易地理解你的意思。有一些 discourse markers 是有特定的含义的，应该在恰当的语境中使用。请看一下例子。

Q: What kinds of pets do people have?

A: ... It seems that the most popular pets now are little dogs, especially poodles, like those fluffy brown ones! I suppose the main reason for this is that poodles are relatively low-maintenance, **you know**, they don't shed that much fur, unlike big dogs ...

如果你在演讲中使用了 you know，那么就意味着你接下来要说一些众人皆知的事实 universal facts。

下面是错误使用 you know 的一些例子。

Q: What kinds of food do you like?

A: You know, I like Korean barbecue, what else ... oh and sashimi ...

点评：这个回答翻成中文就是“你懂的，我喜欢韩式烧烤”。考官怎么会知道你喜欢韩式烧烤呢？

Q：Which places have you been to in China?

A：I have been to many different places in China，for example，West Lake，you know，the place is as beautiful as heaven ...

点评：作为一个“歪果人”，考官可不一定去过 West Lake，甚至都不一定听说过。所以，当听到“你知道的，西湖的景色如天堂般美丽”，考官可能一头雾水。

Module 3　练习

1. What do you do on weekends?

2. Do you think modern people have enough time for relaxing?

3. Do you prefer to take pictures of people or of scenery?

4. How do you keep your photos?

5. Do you frame any of your photos?

6. Do you prefer to send postcards to people or to send photos that you took yourself?

7. Do you like swimming?

8. Where do (or can) people go swimming in your hometown (or, near your home)?

9. Why do many people like swimming?

10. What do you think are the benefits of swimming (or, the benefits of knowing how to swim)?

11. What do people do on weekend?

12. Do you think people should be asked to work on weekends?

13. What leisure activities do you and your family like doing together?

14. Is there any sport that you have never played that you would like to try?

Part 2 The Long-turn

Module 1 Brainstorming 头脑风暴

◇ Read the examples of a brainstorming exercise. 请看以下头脑风暴的例子。

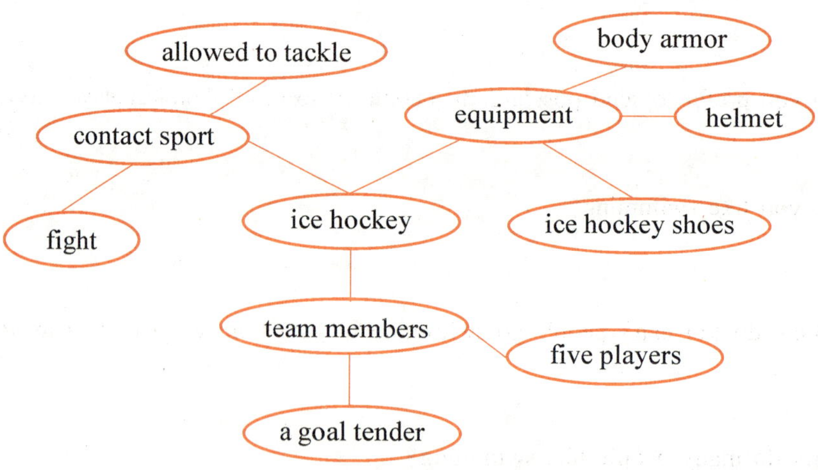

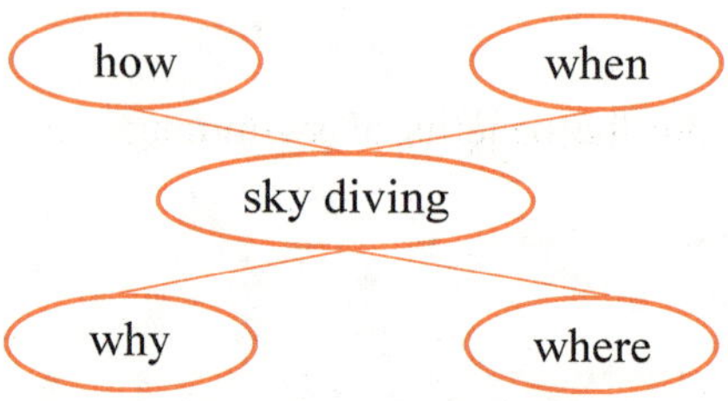

◇ Write down some words or phrases that you can think of to describe the topic given in the center. 脑洞大开，关于以下中心关键词，你能想到从哪些方面描述它，写下来吧。

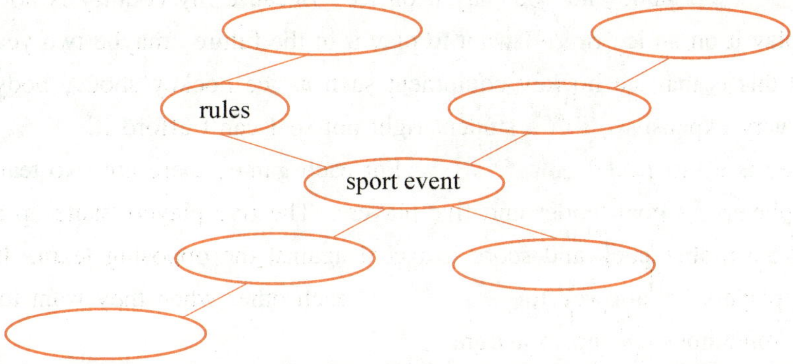

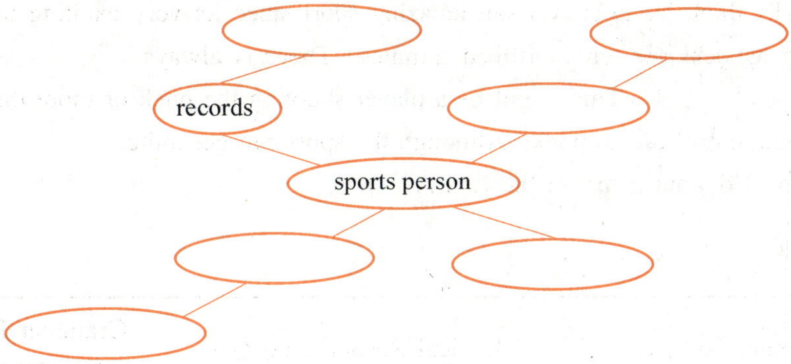

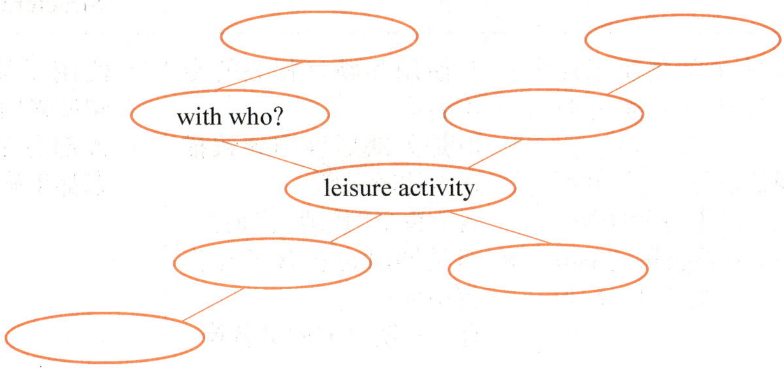

Module 2 实战演练

Describe a sport you'd like to try You should say: what sport it is when you plan to try it how you will try it and explain why you want to try this particular sport

6 分答案

Today I want to describe a sport I would like to try and this sport is Ice hockey. Ice hockey is a fast paced game and you play it on ice. Because my country is not very cold, I will have to play it on an ice rink. I want to play it in the future, maybe two years later. The reason behind this is that ice hockey equipment such as ice hockey shoes, body armour and the helmet is very expensive. I'm a student right not so I can't afford it.

Ice hockey is a fast paced contact sport. For each game, there are two teams, and each team has six players, a goal tender and five players. The five players skate up and down the rink trying take a rubber puck and score it a goal against the opposing team. It is a contact sport because players are allowed to legally tackle each other when they want to fight for the puck and this sometimes end up in a fight.

I personally think ice hockey is an amazing sport since its very exciting unlike football where nothing happens for ten to fifteen minutes. There is always something happening in every minute of the game. This might be a player shooting the puck or more than one player tackling to gain control of the puck. Although the sport can get quite violent and dangerous, it is still a sport I'd want to try in the future.

为什么是 6 分?

Coherence(6 分)	Lexical Resource (6 分)	Grammar Range and Structure (7 分)
× 连接词欠缺 + 重复使用连接词;大部分句子都是简单句。 × 没有出现话语标记;考生可能出现明显的卡可和停顿。 × 回答偏短,未必能超过 part 2 回答要求(至少 1 分 30 秒)。	✓ 有使用和题目相关的专用名词。 × 但是欠缺形容词导致描述点比较跳跃。 ✓ 展示少量“接地气”词汇。 × 但是同时也包含了写作应用词汇。 ✓ 有展示明显的同义替换。	✓ 使用了简单和复杂句型来回答问题。 ✓ 大部分的句子和时态都正确。

高分词汇

fast paced 节奏明快
contact sport 身体接触的体育项目
legally tackle 合法碰撞
something happening 都会有事情发生
every minute of the game 比赛的每一分钟
violent and dangerous 暴力和危险

高分答案

Right, so I'd like to talk about a sport I haven't participated before but I'd like to try in the future and this sport is skydiving. Skydiving is an extreme sport. Divers take an aeroplane high up into the sky, around 16000 ft. And jump off. After they jump, they'd free-fall for around 5-10 minutes and if there is more than one skydiver, they can fly towards each other, grab each other's arms and legs and create different patterns in the sky. When the divers reach a certain altitude, they'll have to pull out their parachutes hanging in the air for a while as they slowly descend towards their landing spot.

Moving onto when and where I'd like to try this sport. Skydiving requires ample space for planes to take off and set down as well as a safe area for skydivers to land. If I want to try this sport, I'll have to travel outside my country, maybe to Australia or the U. K. I only know a few countries so I'll have to do a little more research. Now, I might able to try out this sport in the not too distant future since I'm planning to study in the U. K. and I know a lot of British universities organise skydiving clubs and skydiving events so I guess it's pretty easy to have a crack at.

Now finally, if I have time, I'd like to explain why skydiving is the sport I wanna try. I still remember around 10 years ago when I was completing secondary school project, I manage to come across a skydiving programme on my television. I thought the skydivers in the programme were really cool and the best thing they mentioned about skydiving is that they felt "as free as a bird". I've always wanted to fly in the sky like a bird and skydiving is the closest thing to flying. That's why I can say skydiving is a sport I'd like to try.

点评–为什么高分?

Coherence(7 分)	Lexical Resource (7 分)	Grammar Range and Structure (7 分)
✓ 能适当展开话题,每段思路明显。 ✓ 能灵活和准确使用多元化的连接词和信号词。 × 回答可能偏短;能超过 1 分 30 秒但是未必能到 2 分钟;话题未能完全扩展。	✓ 使用了中高级词汇和比较地道的习语和俚语。 ✓ 可以使用更多的专用名词和相关的形容词来更准确地描述话题。 ✓ 多次出现同义替换。	✓ 多次使用复杂结构来准确展开话题和保持连贯性。 ✓ 没有明显的语法和时态错误,准确度极高。

高分词汇

participated 参与
extreme sport 极限运动
ample space 足够的位子
take off 起飞
set down 降落
not too distant future 在不久的将来
pretty easy to have a crack at 蛮容易开始/尝试
come across 偶然发现
as free as a bird 好像一只鸟那么自由
closest thing 最类似

Describe an extracurricular activity you do/did in school.
You should say:
what the activity is/was
who you do/did it with
when and where you do/did it
and explain how you feel/felt about it.

6 分答案

I want to talk about an extracurricular activity I do in school and this activity is drama club. My school's drama club is usually held in the main hall where there is lots of space for students to move around. If we have to perform, there is also a stage with professional light and sound equipment to assist us. I usually attend this club two times a week, every Tuesday and Thursday. But if we have to prepare for a performance, I sometimes go to the club four times a week after I finish my lessons.

Now, as for what the drama club is about, the drama club is lead by the head teacher of the drama department and the aim is to learn different acting skills and perform it to an audience from time to time. We would usually wear a black t-shirt which is the standard dress code for the club and take on different roles using simple accessories such as a feather or a hat. Through learning different acting skills, I learnt how to control my emotions and how to express myself using different body languages and hand gestures.

Personally speaking, the drama club is a great way to release my stress after a long day of school. I can forget who I am for a while whilst I get involved with the character I'm acting as. What's more, because I'm a shy person, I can actually become confident by performing in front of a live audience without worrying I will do something stupid. I hope to continue this activity in the future and hope to become a professional actor if I had to chance to do so.

为什么是 6 分?

Coherence(7 分)	Lexical Resource (6 分)	Grammar Range and Structure (7 分)
✓ 出现多种连接词;提高答案的黏性。 × 没有出现话语标记;考生可能出现明显的卡可和停顿。 × 回答偏短,未必能超过 part 2 回答要求(至少 1 分 30 秒)。	✓ 虽然有提供充分的描述词汇。 × 但是个别描述点扩展欠缺。 × 展示少量"接地气"词汇但是同时也包含了写作应用词汇。 ✓ 有展示明显的同义替换。	✓ 使用了简单和复杂句型来回答问题。 ✓ 大部分的句子和时态都正确。

高分词汇

extracurricular activity 课外活动
move around 走来走去
assist us 协助我们/提供协助
control my emotions 控制我的情绪
express myself 表达自己的感情/情绪
get involved 参与其中

高分答案

Ok, this is quite a hard topic for me as I've left school for quite some time now, however I guess I can talk about my chess club which I was really engaged in during my years in secondary school. Hmmm ... I still recall my chess club would meet up every Tuesday after school in the science lab. When we arrived, we had to go to one of the cupboards to collect the chess sets and match clocks and lay it all out on the worktables. At around 3.45, the teachers responsible for the club would lock the doors and we would start our games in absolute silence.

As for who was involved, the chess club mainly consisted of lower secondary students with the odd high school student. I guess it's mainly because a lot of the older students had a lot more homework compared to the younger students and they needed to prepare for the finals which meant they didn't have a lot of time to participate in extracurricular activities. Besides, lower secondary students were required to participate in after school activities if they wanted to attain a high grade in their end of year reports, which I can say was a big thing back then.

Pulling the story back onto myself, I was actually a pretty avid chess player so I'd say I enjoyed every chess club session back in the days. Every game was a battle between great minds so I cherished every interaction between different opponents. However, it wasn't all smooth sailing as sometimes I would lose some close games which left me down in the dumps. But I said to myself, you win some, you lose some so I guess it's all good, haha.

点评-为什么高分?

Coherence(7 分)	Lexical Resource (8 分)	Grammar Range and Structure (8 分)
✓ 能适当展开话题,每段思路明显。 ✓ 能灵活和准确使用多元化的连接词和信号词。 × 回答可能偏短;能超过 1 分 30 秒但是未必能到 2 分钟;话题未能完全扩展。	✓ 使用了多种中高级词汇和地道的习语和俚语;充分展示个别观点和观点相关的感觉。 ✓ 可以使用更多的专用名词和相关的形容词来更准确地描述话题。 ✓ 多次出现同义替换。	✓ 多次使用复杂结构来准确展开话题和保持连贯性。 ✓ 事态统一;能使用复杂度偏高的结构;准确度极高。

高分词汇

left school 毕业
really engaged 相当投入
I still recall 我还记得
absolute silence 绝对的安静
with the odd 单独一两个
big thing back then 在那个时候是个大事件
Pulling the story back onto myself 把故事说回来
avid 有激情
back in the days 想当年
cherished 珍惜的

Module 3 Speech 的结构

雅思口语 Part 2 话题卡上的最后一个问题常常是"why ..."。考生在回答时,可能会提及不只一个原因,那么,除了 because 外,还有哪些表示"原因"的表达呢?

第一个原因As for why ...

第二个原因And I suppose another reason why ...

第三个原因What else is there to say ... um ... Oh yeah, one final thing to mention would be ...

Module 4 练习

TIPS:

为了节约时间,我们在记笔记时要尽量使用缩写。如果考生在考试时临场发挥,在记笔记时当场创造一些缩写符号,可能到了之后演讲的过程中当考生在回过头来看时,已经忘了这些缩写符号代表的含义了。因此,考生应当在备考阶段就开始创造自己的缩写符号,并且每次口语练习时,都使用这些符号,这样到了考生真正上考场时,已经对这些符号非常熟悉了。

◇ Now write your notes within 1 min and then give a speech about it. 计时练习! 一分钟时间记笔记,两分钟时间陈述。

Practice 1

Describe a sports event that you took part in or watched.
You should say:
what the event was (or, what the sport was)
where it was
who was competing
what you did during this competition
and explain how you felt about this event.

Notes:

Practice 2

Describe an interest or hobby that you enjoy.
You should say:
how you became interested in it
how long you have been doing it
why you enjoy it
and explain what benefits you get from this interest or hobby

Notes:

Practice 3

Describe a relaxing day you had once after a period of hard work.
You should say:
when you had this relaxing day
where you spent this day
who you spent it with (and what you did)
and explain why it was relaxing.

Notes:

Practice 4

Describe an indoor game that you played when you were a child.
You should say:
what the game was
where you played it
who you played it with
and explain why you enjoyed this game.

Notes:

Part 3 Discussion

Module 1 考题回顾

本章将 Hobbies 和 Sports 两个话题放在一起,是因为这两个话题是互相关联的,是有重叠部分的。有些考生的 hobby 就是 playing sports。这两个话题可以放在一起准备。以下是 Part 3 部分,Hobbies & Sports 话题中,考官常问的一些问题。

1. Why do some people get obsessed with their hobbies?
2. What benefits do hobbies have on a person's life?
3. Do men and women like the same hobbies?

4. How do you think of extreme sports?

5. Do you think that it is possible to become too competitive in sport? In what way?

6. Do you think gambling on sports event is acceptable?

与 Part 1 不同的是,Part 3 问题往往不是问考生的个人经历,而是问考生对某个社会现象的看法。因此,考生在备考时需要关注一些热门的社会现象,这样才能在考试时有话可说。例如,第 4 题问了考生对极限运动的看法。我们在备考中可以在外文网站输入关键词,搜索出一些相应的报道或评论,在回答问题时就可以借鉴。

网站推荐:

www. theguardian. co. uk

www. thetimes. co. uk

◇ Read the news on *extreme sports* and write your own thoughts about this topic. 阅读下面关于极限运动的新闻,并写出你的观点。

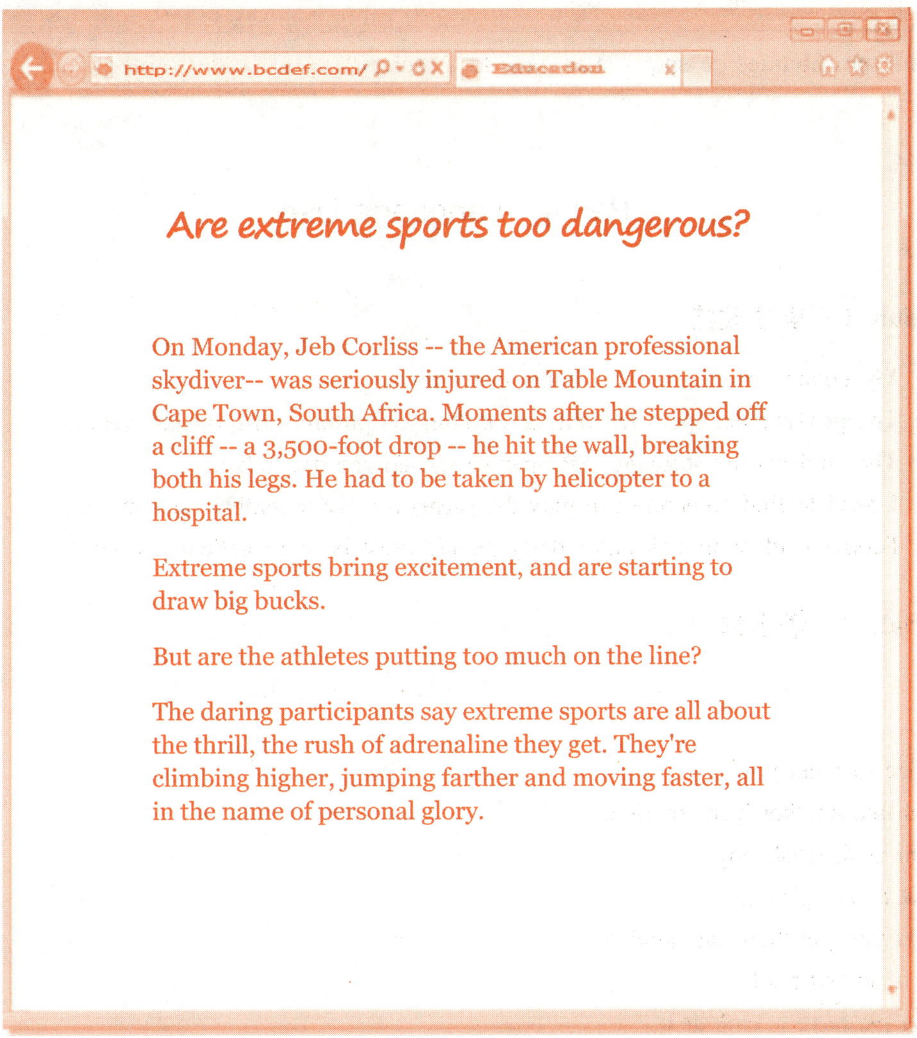

Are extreme sports too dangerous?

On Monday, Jeb Corliss -- the American professional skydiver-- was seriously injured on Table Mountain in Cape Town, South Africa. Moments after he stepped off a cliff -- a 3,500-foot drop -- he hit the wall, breaking both his legs. He had to be taken by helicopter to a hospital.

Extreme sports bring excitement, and are starting to draw big bucks.

But are the athletes putting too much on the line?

The daring participants say extreme sports are all about the thrill, the rush of adrenaline they get. They're climbing higher, jumping farther and moving faster, all in the name of personal glory.

Module 2 Debate & Discussion

Debate: Work in two teams and debate. You have two minutes to think about what you are going to say. 分2组,围绕以下话题,进行辩论。(准备时间:2分钟)

Would you agree that sport stars earn too much money?

Team A

Opinion 1 ________________

Opinion 2 ________________

Opinion 3 ________________

Team B

Opinion 1 ________________

Opinion 2 ________________

Opinion 3 ________________

Discussion: Discuss and answer the question below. 讨论以下话题。

What responsibilities do sports stars have to a society?

Part 4 Language Use

Module 1 语法改错

1. My cousin watch TV for 8 hours every day.
2. The government spent ten millions dollars on public transport last year.
3. The students are studying AP Spanish should see me today.
4. I need to find someone can play the piano for our assembly next month.
5. People work with sick and elderly people must be very patient and kind.

Module 2 语音练习

Direction: link the words with a " ~ " and read aloud. 根据连读规律,连接单词并朗读句子。

Nice to meet you.

I'd like another bowl of rice.

I'm an English boy.

Put it on, please.

Did you get there late again?

It is an old book.

Let me have a look at it.

I called you half an hour ago.
Not at all.
Please pick it up.
Would you like a cup of tea?
Can he do it?
Tell him to ask her . . .
Thank you.
Could you help me, please?

Chapter 5 Media & Technology

话题词汇热身训练

Module 1 词汇

◇ Exercise 1. Make the following into sentences and read the sentences aloud. 用下列单词组成句子并大声朗读。

n.	*v.*	*adj.*
smart phone	panic	addicted
gadget	download	amusing
calculator	upload	informative
signal	interrupt	thrilling
device	promote	horrible
function	operate	convenient
privacy	navigate	humorous
block-buster	boost	vivid
science fiction	make people's life easier	up-to-date
action movie	catch my eyes	effective
cartoon	affect	edgy
romance	encourage	revolutionary
documentary	persuade	classic
billboard	inspire	touching
flyer	show a picture of ...	commercial
touch screen		
director		
panel computer		
consumption		

1. My mobile phone/features/text messaging/games/video calls.

My mobile phone has a lot of features like text messaging, games, camera and even video calls.

2. I/fan/comedies/I/love/everything/laugh.

3. I/prefer/movies/in the cinema/it/offer me/audio and visual enjoyment/special effects.

4. Computer/become/my daily life/it/hard/imagine/how/I/survive without it.

5. Although you/turn mobile phone/mute mode, it/distract/you/classes/reduce/efficiency.

◇ Exercise 2. Write down some words or phrases that you can think of within 30 seconds to answer these questions. And then work in pairs to ask and answer these questions. 流利度达成——30 秒内写出你能想到的可以回答下列问题的单词或词组！并与你身边的同学两人一组互相提问回答这些问题。

1. Do you often read newspapers?

2. What feature (or, function) of your cell phone do you like the best?

3. Do you like to watch films in the cinema or at home?

4. Who is your favorite movie star?

5. What are the different ways people get news?

直击考点

Module 1 Connectives 连接词

Complete the following sentences using although, despite, in spite of, however or though. 用选项中的连接词填空。

1. We went out ________ the rain.
a) despite　　b) in spite of　　c) Either could be used here

2. We went out ________ it was raining.
a) despite　　b) though　　c) Either could be used here

3. The judge sent her to prison ________ the fact that she had very small children.
a) despite　　b) however　　c) although

4. ________ I didn't enjoy the movie, I watched it.

a) Though　　b) Despite

5. I enjoyed the party ________ I didn't know anybody there.

a) though　　b) in spite of

6. I bought the watch, ________ it was expensive.

a) however　　b) though　　c) Either could be used here

7. John didn't come; ________, everybody else did.

a) however　　b) though　　c) Either could be used here

8. ________ the government refuses to admit it, it has failed to revive the economy.

a) Although　　b) Despite　　c) In spite of

9. He failed ________ his hard work.

a) in spite of　　b) though　　c) however

10. I didn't like her rude behavior. ________, I said nothing.

a) However　　b) Despite　　c) Though

Module 2　Paraphrase 词群同义转换

◇ Write down the synonyms of the following words and describe the word to your group members. 写出下列单词的同义词，并用自己话向身边的同学描述这个单词。

Example: impact: influence

✓ have an effect upon

important: ________________________________

____

funny: ________________________________

____

expensive: ________________________________

____

modern: ________________________________

____

Part 1　Interview

Module 1　How often/When ... 时间频率

雅思口语的四项评分标准中，语法是大家往往会忽略或者说觉得很难提高的一项。然而，在考试中，这个评分标准是考官纠错的时候关注最多的。而语法中的时态又是中国考生最容易犯错误的环节。尤其是过去时态,如果经常出现过去时态的错误,那么你的口语基本上是不会拿到5.5分以上了。

在 Part 1 的问答中,考官时常会问到考生"多长时间做某事?"或者"上一次做某件事情是什么时候?"如下:

How often do you write an email or letter?

How often do you travel to the countryside?

When was the last time you did something in a hurry?

How often do you take the bus or taxi?

这两个问题虽然都是与时间相关,但是在回答是需要注意 how often 问的是做某件事的频率,也就是一个一般的惯常的情况,通常用一般现在时就可以。在表达具体一共做过几次时,会使用到现在完成时,如:I've never been to the museum in my hometown. /I've only been abroad for three times.

而上一次做某事明显是关于过去的事情,因此要使用一般过去时。

我们来看看这两种问题分别有哪些句型和词组来回答。

1. How often ...?

➢ 小练习:按表达频率从高到低排列以下的词和词组:

sometimes　　seldom　　once in a while　　never　　hardly

hundreds of times　　every once a year　　quite often

排序:______________________________

2. When was the last time ...?

回答思路:

a. 交代时间:The last time that I did something was ... (two years ago, last month ...)

b. 解释 feeling:

I still clearly remember at that time I was very excited ...

It was absolutely an unforgettable experience in my life ...

I guess it was the first time that I did sth. and also the last time.

Honestly, I didn't really remember ... coz it was just normal.

◇ Exercise. Answer the following questions. 回答下列问题。

1. How often do you use your mobile phone?

2. How often do you watch a movie?

3. When was the last time you went to a cinema?

Module 2 实战演练

➢ Examiner: Do you have a mobile phone?

No doubt. Everyone can't live without a mobile phone. I use it every day and I just realize that I'm kind of mobile phone addict these days. I use it on my way to the office sending text messages. And I use it to watch video clips on Youtube while I was waiting for someone. It's just indispensable.

➢ Examiner: Which do you prefer reading, magazines or newspapers?

I think I prefer reading newspapers coz it's obviously more informative. Plus it's getting harder to find a newsstand so I barely buy any magazines anymore. And you can get newspapers on some public transportation like subway and airplane. And it's lighter to carry with me. So I prefer newspapers.

➢ Examiner: When did you get your first mobile phone?

As far as I still remember, I got my first mobile phone as a 16 years old birthday gift. It's a Samsung, white color. I was so excited to have it that I kept it with me all day long. I remember I often played a type pet game on it. It's not a smart phone so you know, the games on it were all old-school.

➢ Examiner: Do you like watching films?

Definitely, I'm a huge fan of science fiction. I watch nearly every Marvel's movie in the cinema. I'm so addicted to those special effects and the fighting movements. It's so cool. And when I'm at home alone I'll probably choose some romance and family theme stories. I think watching movies is a good way to relieve stress.

➢ Examiner: How does the news affect people?

Well I guess news has an impact on people in terms of their expectations about the future. People get to know what's going on in the world through news. For example, many people pay a lot of attention on the health care, because they are thinking about their future life quality.

➢ Examiner: What types of TV programmes do you (most) like to watch?

Normally I don't watch TV programs that often nowadays. I watch some American TV series online like Game of Thrones, Modern Family and Two Broke Girls. I watch them to kill time and at the same time gain some authentic expressions in English. Game of Thrones is really good. It's terrific.

Discourse Markers

本章我们介绍以下 2 个 discourse markers:

I mean ... 我的意思是……

..., which means that ... 这就意味着……

在演讲时,考生常常会先提出一个总的观点,接下来会对这个观点进行详细的解释说明。I mean ... 和...，which means that ... 这 2 个 discourse markers 都表示说话的人接下来要进行解释说明了。

例如：

Q：Do you like birds?

A：Yes，I'd say birds are lovely creatures. **I mean**，they look graceful when they fly，especially pigeon and skylark ...

是的。我认为鸟儿是很美好的生物。我的意思是，它们飞起来的时候看上去非常优雅，尤其是鸽子和云雀……

解析：they look graceful when they fly 是对 birds are lovely creatures 的解释说明。

Q：What type of newspaper do you prefer to read?

A：... It calls itself an independent newspaper，**which means that** it does not give its support to a particular political party ...

……它自称为一份独立的报纸，这就意味着它不支持任何一个政治党派……

解析：it does not give its support to a particular political party 是对 It calls itself an independent newspaper 的解释说明。

Module 3 练习

1. Do you prefer reading a newspaper，or watching TV?

2. How do you feel about advertisements on TV?

3. Do you use computers very much?

4. Is your cell phone important for you in your daily life?

5. How did you feel when you got your first mobile phone?

6. Do you like reading?

7. Do you think there's too much advertising in our daily lives?

8. What kinds of products do you think are most suitable to be advertised?

9. What impact on people does music in advertisements have?

10. What is the purpose of advertising?

Part 2 The Long-turn

Module 1 Brainstorming 头脑风暴

◇ Read the examples of a brainstorming exercise. 请看以下头脑风暴的例子。

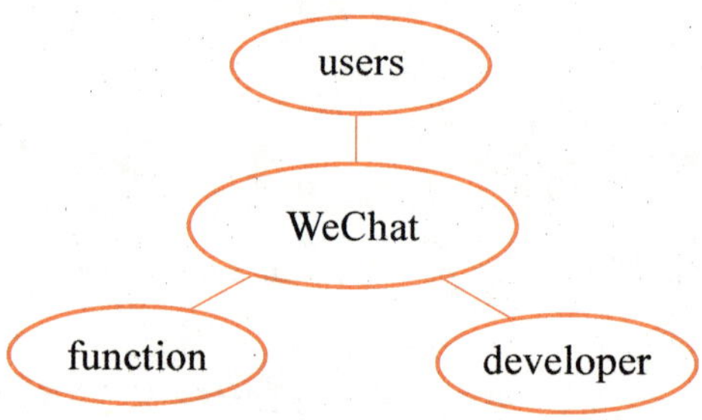

news: ATM heist
where I read it: local newspaper
my feeling about the news: shocked
What I learnt from the article: I could contribute my two-cents on the matter

◇ Write down some words or phrases that you can think of to describe the topic given in the center. 脑洞大开，关于以下中心关键词，你能想到从哪些方面描述它，写下来吧。

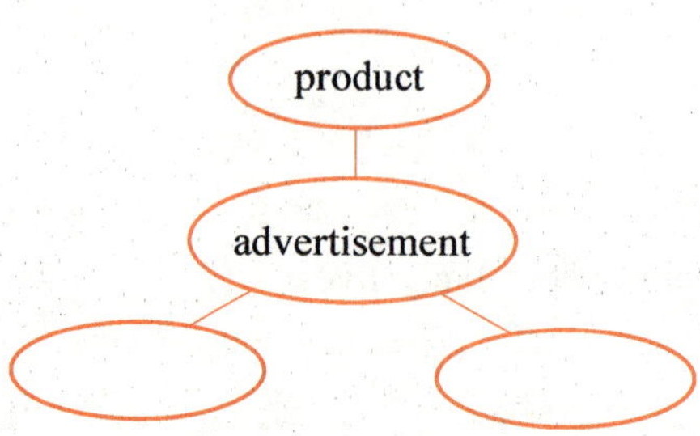

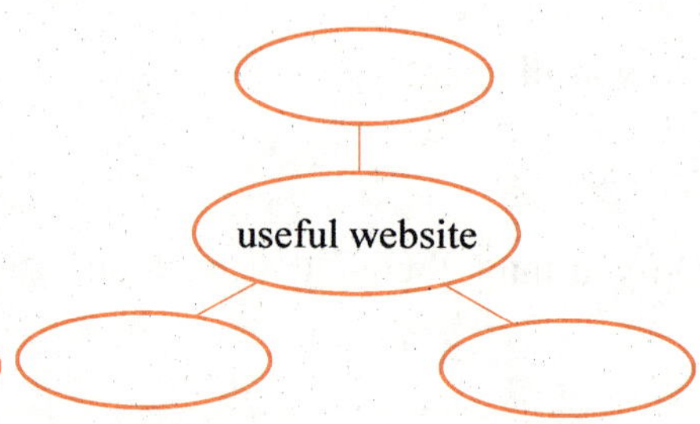

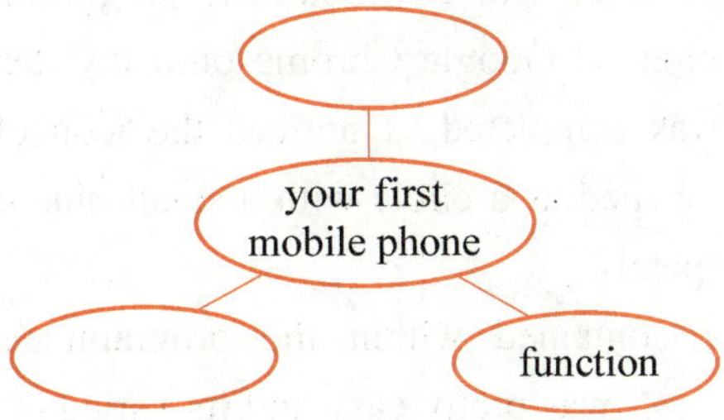

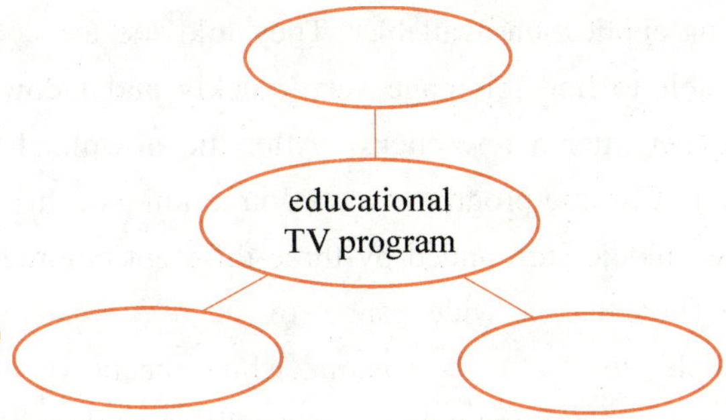

Module 2 实战演练

> Describe a program or app on your computer or phone
> You should say:
> what this app/program is
> how to use it
> why you use this app/program
> and explain how the app/program influences your life.

题目思路和方向(idea brainstorm)

这是一个两层问题(2-tier question)所以必须找出这个 part 2 问题的**两个关键词组**才能满足考官对考生答案的要求。一起通过一些问题和有用的理念来热热身吧:

1. Program or APP:什么 program or APP?能否描述一下图标?有什么功能?什么时候会用?和类似的 program or APP 有什么不一样?

a) WeChat/QQ messenger — Used for instant messaging.

b) Internet explorer/Good Chrome/Safari — Used for surfing the internet.

c) Microsoft word/excel/power point — Used to complete projects/essays/presentations.

2. On computer or phone:为什么出现在你的电脑/手机?怎么下载?带来什么好处和坏处?

6 分答案

Today I'd like to describe a program on my computer and this programme is called Google Chrome. This programme was developed by the multinational company Google and the main function of this programme is that it allows you to surf the internet. When you open the programme you will see a page with an empty bar on top. You type in the internet address of the page you want to visit and when you press enter, the specific page will load.

I still remember using Google Chrome for the first time around three years ago. I was using internet explorer at the time and my friends told me that there was a better internet surfing application available. They told me to access a page to download the programme. I was able to find this page very quickly and I downloaded Google Chrome onto my desktop computer after a few clicks. After the download was completed, I noticed the icon of the Google Chrome programme was quite unique. It is shaped as a circle with a small blue circle in the middle surrounded by three different colored petals.

There are a wide range of positive features contained within the programme, for example, its minimalistic nature which meant navigating was pretty easy and its varied add-on features that assisted me in a many different things such as saving my passwords automatically and blocking pop-ups from random websites. However, the best thing about the programme is its loading speed. It is five times faster than any similar programmes and that means I can view any website within 10 seconds.

高分词汇

Developed 开发/研制
surf the internet 游览网页
access 进入
positive features 好的特征
navigating 导航/使用
add-on features 附加功能

为什么是6分?

Coherence(6分)	Lexical Resource (6分)	Grammar Range and Structure (6分)
✓ 使用多种句内连接。 × 但是欠缺句和句之间的连接。 ✓ 回答长度可接收,能超过1分30秒的基本要求。	✓ 有使用和题目相关的专用名词。 × 但是欠缺形容词导致描述点比较跳跃。 ✓ 展示少量"接地气"词汇。 × 但是同时也包含了写作应用词汇。 ✓ 有展示明显的同义替换。	× 简单句为主,少数复杂句。 ✓ 大部分的句子和时态都正确。

高分答案

Right, there are a number of APPs I can talk about but the one I'd particularly like to mention is an instant messaging APP called WeChat. WeChat is a smart phone based APP created by the Chinese conglomerate "Tencent" and appeared on the Chinese market in 2013 which was basically a time when the demand for on-the-go communication was at its peak. It has gained popularity over the years due to its ease of use and its variety of functions, and now millions of users treat this APP as their main communication tool whether it is for day to day communication or work based communication.

Now, I'm going to talk about this APP from a more personal standpoint. This APP basically sits in the communications folder on my cutting edge smart phone and it appears as a little green square with two speech bubbles in the middle. When I double-tap into it, I can see on my conversations I've had in the past as well as discussion groups that I've set up between my friends and my work mates. The best thing about this discussion group function is that I can pass on my message to various people at a time instead of talking to them one by one.

Besides chit chatting with other people using this APP, I also utilize its wide range of add-on functions to assist me with my day-to-day chores. For example, when I want to top-up my phone, all I need to do is to punch in my phone number and huala! All done! Furthermore, when I want to travel by train or if I want to travel further by plane, I can easily purchase tickets at a pretty reasonable price without running to the travel agency every time.

So, from what I know, WeChat is always upgrading its services to satisfy its users' needs and that's why I'll continue to use this APP in the foreseeable future.

高分词汇

smart phone based APP 智能电话的应用程序
appeared on the Chinese market 出现在中国的市场
on-the-go communication 活动式沟通方法
gained popularity 增加/获得更加多的欢迎
cutting edge 最新的/创新的
double-tap 按两次
pass on 交代/交流
chit chatting 闲聊
day-to-day chores 日常需要处理的东西

点评-为什么高分?

Coherence(8 分)	Lexical Resource (8 分)	Grammar Range and Structure (8 分)
✓ 能适当展开话题,每段思路明显。 ✓ 能灵活和准确使用多元化的连接词和信号词。 ✓ 回答详细;能达到 2 分钟的最高要求。	✓ 使用了中高级词汇和多种地道的习语和俚语。 ✓ 使用多种专用名词和相关的形容词来更准确地描述话题。 ✓ 多次出现同义替换。	✓ 多次使用复杂结构来准确展开话题和保持连贯性。 ✓ 没有明显的语法和时态错误,准确度极高。

Describe an article that you read from a magazine or newspaper
You should say:

> what the article was
> when and where you read it
> what you learnt from the article
> and explain why you think it is a good or bad article.

题目思路和方向(idea brainstorm)

这是一个两层问题(2-tier question)所以必须找出这个 part 2 问题的**两个关键词组**才能满足考官对考生答案的要求。一起通过一些问题和有用的理念来热热身吧：

1. An article you read：什么 Article？谁编写的？描述一下内容？看完后有什么感受？会因为看完这个 article 改变一些东西吗？

2. Magazine or newspaper：什么 magazine or newspaper？在什么情况下看这个 magazine or newspaper？是常常看的吗？

a) Cosmopolitan — A lighthearted fashion magazine aimed at young female readers.

b) National Geographic — One of the most well known magazines in the world. A periodical that talks about social, historical, natural, and cultural events around the world.

c) Times Magazine — A famous magazine that focuses on economic, political, and social issues.

d) China Daily — An English language based newspaper that talks about Chinese policies, events, and Chinese cultural affairs.

6 分答案

Today, I'm going to describe an article I read in a magazine. Last month, I read an article in a health-care magazine, called Healthy Living, which left me with a deep impression. This article was written by a young university student who became an internet superstar after she shared how she lost 92 kilograms in a year. She was very fat before but now, not only is she slim, but also very fit. According to the author, she tried to lose weight before by trying quick-fix diets. Instead of losing weight, she actually gained more weight. Because of this, she decided quit quick-fix diets and attempt a more normal diet routine.

She said in her article that we should eat grain foods like sweet corn and wheat products if we hope to keep fit. We are also supposed to drink two cups of warm water after we wake up as this helps with our body's metabolism. Furthermore, she mentioned that we should not rely on fruit juices or vegetable juices to lose weight. This is because by grinding the fruits and vegetables, a lot of the nutrition is broken down and that's why we should eat whole fruits and vegetables instead.

After reading the article, I felt like I was able to lose weight in a healthier way now since I used to think if I want to lose weight, I had to eat as little as possible. However, this article told me that I can still lose weight and maintain my figure without avoiding dinner. Furthermore, the author's selfie of herself before she lost weight and after she lost weight gave me a lot of motivation to try her ideas out.

高分词汇

deep impression 印象深刻
internet superstar 网络明星
According to the author 按作者所写的
mentioned 提起
selfie 自拍
motivation 动力

为什么是 6 分?

Coherence(7 分)	Lexical Resource (6 分)	Grammar Range and Structure (6 分)
✓ 使用多连接词;提高答案黏性。 ✓ 结构明确;答案有条理地发展。 × 回答比较短;有可能不达到最基本的 1 分 30 秒要求。	✓ 有使用和题目相关的专用名词。 × 但是欠缺形容词导致描述点比较跳跃。 ✓ 展示少量"接地气"词汇。 × 但是同时也包含了写作应用词汇。 ✓ 有展示明显的同义替换。	× 简单句为主,少数复杂句。 ✓ 大部分的句子和时态都正确。

高分答案

Ok, to tell you the truth, I don't have much to say on articles in a magazine or newspapers since I prefer to get my daily dose of information through news programmes on the television. But, I'll do my best to talk about an article about an ATM heist which I came across whilst casually reading a local newspaper on the underground.

Now, as for what the news was about, I still remember it mentioned something along the lines of a national manhunt for criminals that looted millions of dollar from my hometown's cash machines in an hour-long heist. These criminals were armed with fake credit card details from a well known national bank and they hit over 1,400 ATM machines in a coordinated attack. There were around 100 people? I don't really remember the exact details but what they did was made multiple withdrawals each within a three hour window which meant they hauled in around eight million pounds by the time they ended their operation.

I was actually pretty shocked after reading this article since I work as an operations manager in a bank myself and this news actually caused quite a stir within the banking sector that day. What was surprising is that all the banks in my hometown have withdrawal limit of around six hundred pounds per day but the gang managed to bypass this limit and made off with millions of dollars so quickly without setting off any alarms.

The funny thing is, after reading this article, my director scheduled an emergency meeting in response to this particular news since he had doubts about our bank's own ATM system and he wanted to see if there were any possibilities of this happening to our own ATM machines. I guess it was a good thing I read about it before I went to work since I knew what happened and I could contribute my two-cents on the matter.

高分词汇

daily dose 每天必须做的
came across 遇到的
casually reading 休闲地阅读
mentioned something along the lines of 好像提过的
pretty shocked 蛮惊讶的
caused quite a stir 引起骚动
funny thing is 搞笑的是
it was a good thing 是一件好事
I could contribute my two-cents 提供我小小的意见

点评–为什么高分?

Coherence(8 分)	Lexical Resource (8 分)	Grammar Range and Structure (8 分)
✓ 能适当展开话题,每段思路明显。 ✓ 能灵活和准确使用多元化的连接词和信号词。 ✓ 回答详细;能达到 2 分钟的最高要求。	✓ 使用了中高级词汇和多种地道的习语和俚语。 ✓ 使用多种专用名词和相关的形容词来更准确地描述话题。 ✓ 多次出现同义替换。	✓ 多次使用复杂结构来准确展开话题和保持连贯性。 ✓ 没有明显的语法和时态错误,准确度极高。

Module 3　Speech 的结构

在雅思口语 Part 2 环节,考生结束演讲时可以用眼神向考官示意自己已经说完了。也可以直接跟考官说:

So, yeah, I guess that's pretty much everything there is to say, so thanks a lot for listening.

或者

So, yeah, this is basically why + 总结一下之前说的理由. Thanks for listening.

或者

So yeah, this is pretty much what + 总结一下之前说的内容. Thanks for listening.

Module 4 练习

TIPS:

在 Part 2 环节,谈到一件事的流程时,考生常常会用到"首先……;接下来……;然后……;最后……"这个结构,用箭头来表示流程,会比写字快得多,可以节约宝贵的准备时间。请看以下例子。

浪费时间的 notes:

go diving

First . . . rent equipment

After that . . . warm-up: stretch arms and legs (10mins)

Then . . . trained by a professional diver (30mins)

Lastly . . . go diving by myself (30mins)

节约时间的 notes:

go diving

rent equipment

warm-up: stretch arms and legs (10mins)

trained by a professional diver (30mins)

go diving by myself (30mins)

◇ Now write your notes within 1 min and then give a speech about it. 计时练习!一分钟时间记笔记,两分钟时间陈述。

Practice 1

Describe an unforgettable advertisement

You should say:

where you saw or heard it

what kind of advertisement it was

what the contents of the advertisement were (or, what product or service was advertised)

and explain how you felt when you saw or heard this advertisement/why you like it

Notes:

Practice 2

Describe a story or novel that was particularly interesting to you
you should say:
what story or the novel was
where you knew it
when you read it
and how you felt about it

Notes:

Practice 3

Describe a problem with an equipment that you couldn't solve.
you should say:
what the equipment was
what the problem was
what you did
and explain how you felt when you couldn't solve the problem

Notes:

Practice 4

Describe your first mobile phone. you should say: when you got it how you got it what you used it for and explain how you felt when you got it.

Notes:

Part 3 Discussion

Module 1 考题回顾

本章将 Media 和 Technology 两个话题放在一起,是因为这两个话题是互相关联的,是有重叠部分的。有些 Media(例如: TV, Internet, etc.)就是 technological invention。这两个话题可以放在一起准备。以下是 Part 3 部分,Media & Technology 话题中考官常问的一些问题。

1. Do you think that modern scientific inventions have really improved our lives?
2. In your opinion, what is the greatest technological invention? Why?
3. What do you think about GMO (genetically modified organisms) vegetables?
4. What are the main media outlets in China today?
5. What are some of the main differences between getting information from magazines and getting information from other media such as TV or the internet?
6. How could we avoid unreliable information appearing on the internet?

在雅思口语考试中,提到"科技"这个话题往往会问到科技对个人、对社会的影响。

例如，第 1 题问了考生对“科技发明是否改善人们生活?”我们在备考中可以在外文网站输入关键词，搜索出一些相应的评论，在回答问题时就可以借鉴。

网站推荐：

www. debate. org

www. yahoo. com

◇ Read the debate on *have advances in technology improved our lives* and write your own thoughts about this topic. 阅读下面关于“科技进步是否改善了我们的生活”的辩论，并写出你的观点。

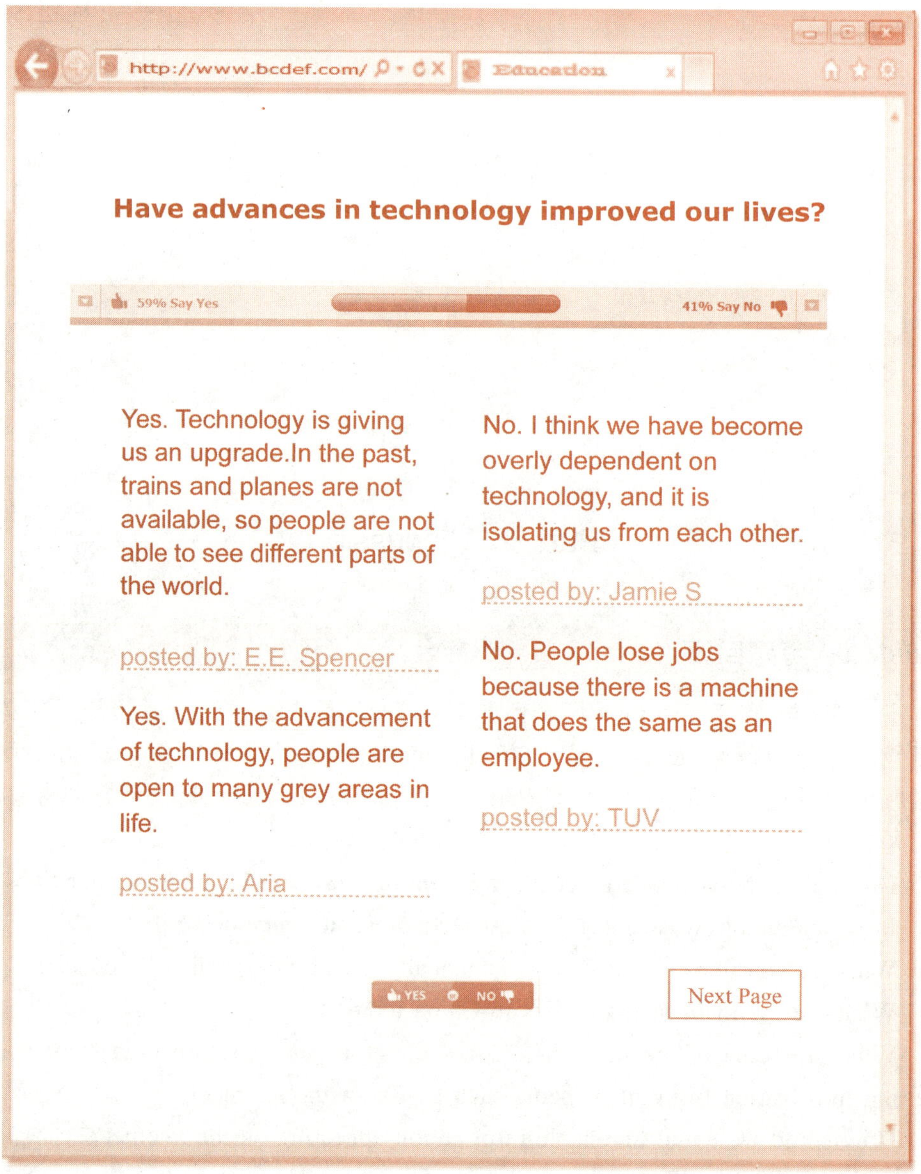

Module 2 Debate & Discussion

Debate: Work in two teams and debate. You have two minutes to think about what you are going to say. 分2组,围绕以下话题,进行辩论。(准备时间:2分钟)

Do you think watching TV is a good way to get information?

Team A

Opinion 1 ______________________

Opinion 2 ______________________

Opinion 3 ______________________

Team B

Opinion 1 ______________________

Opinion 2 ______________________

Opinion 3 ______________________

Discussion: Discuss and answer the question below. 讨论以下话题。

What are the advantages of technology?

Part 4 Language Use

Module 1 语法改错

1. The number of woman studying physics increased dramatically last year.
2. I don't have many time to complete my homework.
3. These days, more and more people traveling to foreign countries for their holidays.
4. I am hoping it is not too late to save endangered animals.
5. There is a pan of porridge and are some bowls in the kitchen.

Module 2 语音练习

Direction: link the words with a " ~ " and read aloud. 根据连读规律,连接单词并朗读句子。

Where are your brother and sister?

I am a student.

She wants to study English.

The question is too easy for him to answer.

Is it a hat or a cat?

She can't carry it.

There is a good book in my desk.

She opened the door and walked in.

I looked for it here and there.

There is a football under it.

Here are four eggs.

Shall we meet at eight or ten tomorrow morning?

But where is my cup?

Chapter 6 Transportation & Environment

话题词汇热身训练

Module 1 词汇

◇ Exercise 1. Make the following into sentences and read the sentences aloud. 用下列单词组成句子并大声朗读。

n.	*v.*	*adj.*
climate	slow down	humid
bloom	bother	crowded
weather forecast	commute	congested
coach	tackle	dusty
lake	ride a bike	cozy
pond	get around	freezing
landscape	suffer from	windy
passenger	chop down	gloomy
route	reflect	urban
guidebook	go fishing	fast-paced
spot	be stuck in	tranquil
farm	happen	amazing
leaf		clear
brunch		foggy
trunk		rainy
lily		windy
bicycle lane		cloudless
oxygen		

1. Congest/become/a daily frustration/urban centers/grow.

2. We/comply/a list of/NYC's coolest secret spot, ones/you're/not/likely/read about/in guidebooks.

3. There/an abundance of/park and garden/close to/the CBD/a variety of common and rare species.

4. Most of us/busy/these days/we/hardly/have the time/enjoy/simple things in life.

5. Smog/hang over/city/is/the most familiar and obvious form/air pollution.

◇ Exercise 2. Write down some words or phrases that you can think of within 30 seconds to answer these questions. And then work in pairs to ask and answer these questions. 流利度达成——30 秒内写出你能想到的可以回答下列问题的单词或词组！并与你身边的同学两人一组互相提问回答这些问题。

1. Are there many parks or public gardens where you live?

2. Describe the four seasons in your hometown.

3. What kind(s) of transport do you usually use?

4. Have you ever been to the countryside?

5. What kinds of people ride bicycles?

直 击 考 点

Module 1 Connectives 连接词

Insert the following connectives into the sentences to make them more logical and coherent. 将下列连接词插入句子中使句子更加完整连贯。

but	however	in contrast	unfortunately	still	nevertheless	... though

1. It's a difficult job, I enjoy it.

2. I was looking forward to a pleasant journey, it turned out a nightmare because of the storm.

3. Many subway stations let you cross the platform to change from one route to another. At times trains leave before customers can make the connection

4. The west coast of North Uist, Benbecula and South Uist are dominated by extensive areas of white-sanded beaches. The east coasts of North and South Uist have a mix of extensive moorland, hills and long narrow sea lochs.

5. The weather reports said it's gonna be boiling hot in the next few days, we were excited about going on a road trip.

6. Beijing is so large that visitors might find it a bit annoying to travel from one destination to another. Public transport will get you to most of the main tourist sites.

7. My flight was delayed to the late evening. Nobody came to explain to us.

Module 2 Paraphrase 词群同义转换

◇ Write down the synonyms of the following words and describe the word to your group members. 写出下列单词的同义词，并用自己话向身边的同学描述这个单词。

Example：underground：tube，subway，metro

✓ an underground electric railroad

kind（种类）：________________

____

quiet：________________

____

a lot of：________________

____

safe：________________

____

Part 1 Interview

Module 1 Which ... What kind of ...？具体种类

这类题型可能是考生在考场上被问到最容易词穷的。因为考官的问题非常具体，需要考生对于某个话题有一定的词汇量，或者又复习准备。例如：

What kind of trees is popular in your country?

这题对很多考生来说难度相对较大，正是因为题目非常具体地涉及了树的种类。如果考前没有复习准备这个话题，那么在考试时说出有营养的内容或者说切题的答案就是比较困难的。当然如果你知道 pine trees（松树）、cypress（柏树）、willow（柳树）、cedar（杉树)、coconut trees(可可树)、palm trees(棕榈树)、rubber trees(橡胶树)这些单词的话,这个题就相对简单,可以迎刃而解了。

Sample: Since China is a large county, the genre of trees is quite different from region to region. Like in the north part, there are more like pine trees and cypress and stuff, while in my hometown and other region we have willow and some palm trees. And my favorite of them is definitely palm trees. Coz it always brings me a feeling that I'm on vacation or what.

回答这类问题时,我们可以采用如上这个例子的总分的形式,也就是先举例说说话题相关的具体有哪些种类,再重点解释强调自己喜欢或者答案的类型:

In general:

There is a bunch of ...

I've tried ... before ...

In most cases, ... is commonly accepted.

On the whole ...

Specific:

I love ... more than any other ...

Among them ... is my favorite without doubt.

Tip:如果在考试中遇到的话题你确实在备考中遗漏了,不要慌张,我们可以用打太极的方式跟考官先周旋一下,然后试着描述这个虽然说不出名字(you can't name it)的话题。

例如:Wow, there really are a lot of different tress. But I never paid attention to their names in English. Like in my hometown there are a lot of trees with long leaves and people normally plant them around a lake or a pond. It looks really romantic especially in spring.

◇ Exercise. Answer the following questions. 回答下列问题。

1. Which is your most/least favorite season?

2. What kinds of animals as a pet do the people have in your country?

3. What kinds of people ride bicycles?

4. Do you like flowers?

Module 2 实战演练

➤ Examiner: Do you like traveling by train?

Sure. I love traveling by train since I was a kid especially for some long distance trip.

The longest one that I had was a trip to Xinjiang. We started from Nanjing. As I remember it took us at least say 3 days to arrive there. It was a trip with another two families so there were three kids including me. The trip was awesome coz we enjoyed very different landscapes and views along the trip.

➢ Examiner: Has the weather in your country changed much in the past few years?

Not that much in my area I guess. My hometown lies in the center of China and the only change might be the temperature. It gets hotter in summer. However, in some large cities like Beijing and Shanghai the air condition turns down to a huge problem. But it's more of a climate problem I guess. The weather reported many gloomy and dusty days in the past three years.

➢ Examiner: Would you prefer to have the same climate all year, or a place that has different seasons?

I'll definitely choose a place with distinctive seasons, coz it's just too boring to live in a place with the same type of climate all year long. Then I'll probably lose the enjoyment to have ice-cream in scorching summer or no snow fight. I don't wanna miss any of them.

➢ Examiner: Have you ever been a place without sunshine?

No. Never. Honestly I can't even think of any in this condition. Perhaps in north pole or south pole? Oh yeah I remembered a picture taken by my friend in Norway. It was during the polar night. Otherwise in most places on earth I guess there must be at least some sunshine even if it's pouring rain or under a really bad weather condition.

➢ Examiner: How do you think the transport system could be improved?

We should move towards electronic vehicles in terms of protecting the air quality. And at the same time upgrade infrastructures in rural areas and provide more public transport routes.

➢ Examiner: What are some well-known natural places in your country?

The first one comes into my mind is the world widely famous Yellow Mountains coz it's nearby my hometown city. Unfortunately I haven't been there yet. What a shame. It's famous for different shapes of rocks and some of them are similar to animal shapes or some other objects, which is cool.

Discourse Markers

我们知道,雅思口语考试的话题会涉及生活的方方面面,考生需要根据不同的话题,表达自己的认识或看法。

有的时候,考生对自己的某些认识并没有十足的把握,或者考生并不能保证自己的认识或看法是百分百正确的。遇到这种情况时,考生们不必担心。因为考生并不需要给出"完全正确"的答案。在雅思口语考试中,考生完全可以表达自己的猜想,这时,可以使用以下 2 个 discourse markers:

If I'm not mistaken, ...

I guess ...

我们来看一下 If I'm not mistaken 和 I guess 的实际运用：

Q：What kinds of pets do people have?

A：... These days little dogs are the most popular, especially poodles. I guess the reason for this is that poodles are adorable, unlike big dogs which seem to be scary.

Q：Do birds have special meanings in China?

A：... For example, Mandarin ducks, if I'm not mistaken, are the symbol of love and commitment in Chinese culture.

用 If I'm not mistaken 和 I guess 表示自己对接下来要说的内容并不是十分确定，在考试中，这样会使答案显得更加真实，因为没有人会对每个话题都持有十分确定的看法！

Module 3 练习

1. Do you like to visit natural places?

2. Is it important to plant trees?

3. Do you think parks are important to a city?

4. What's your favourite animal?

5. Do you like living in the countryside?

6. How old were you when you first learned to ride a bicycle?

7. What's the weather usually like in your hometown?

Part 2 The Long-turn

Module 1 Brainstorming 头脑风暴

◇ Read the examples of a brainstorming exercise. 请看以下头脑风暴的例子。

I was on my way to school (by bus)

↓

a commotion happened

↓

2 cars bumped

↓

I was stuck in a long line

↓

I was late for my exams

↓

cycled across the US (to raise money for charity)

↓

training and preparation for month

↓

begin the journey in July 2010

↓

cycled across mountains, deserts and rivers

↓

camped almost every night

↓

cycled 7,000 km in 49 days

↓

raised over 4,000 pounds for charity

◇ Write down some words or phrases that you can think of to describe the topic given in the center. 脑洞大开，关于以下中心关键词，你能想到从哪些方面描述它，写下来吧。

a means of public transport

↓

↓

↓

↓

a vehicle I would like to buy

↓

↓

↓

↓

an environmental law in your country

↓

↓

↓

↓

an environmental issue that you think is important to focus

Module 2 实战演练

Describe a time when you were stuck in traffic
you should say:
when it happened
where it happened
how you passed the time while waiting
and explain how you felt when you were in that traffic jam.

题目思路和方向(idea brainstorm)

这是一个两层问题(2-tier question),所以必须找出这个 part 2 问题的**两个关键词组**才能满足考官对考生答案的要求。一起通过一些问题和有用的理念来热热身吧:

1. Stuck in traffic:什么交通工具?当时要去干吗?为什么会选这个交通工具?你坐这个交通工具路过哪里?

a) Bus — public transport; economical; convenient; bus stop near where I live/want to go

b) Taxi — in a rush; comfortable; no need to share with other people; meant to be quick and fast.

c) Car — private transport; flexible schedule; adjust route according to traffic conditions

2. A time:为什么会拥堵?当时发生什么事;看到、听到、闻到什么?当时什么感受?

6 分答案

Today I'm going to talk about a time I was stuck in traffic. I can still remember it was about a year ago when I was caught in a traffic jam on my way to the school to attend my thesis debate, which was really important as it was going to affect my overall GPA. I thought at that moment there must have been a severe car crash or something in front. I waited for about thirty minutes, but I could not sense any sign of the flow moving a little bit. Obviously I was anxious since the debate session was about to start in fifteen minutes.

I was really so angry at that time because I actually left my apartment ahead of schedule. In fact, I thought about jumping out of the taxi and walk along the top of all other vehicles to get to my destination. After this miserable halt ended, the taxi zoomed to the conference hall where the debate was held, but unfortunately I was 10 minutes late.

After this scary experience, I always choose to take the subway. Although in rush hours, there are so many people in carriages, the underground train services are mostly on time. I won't be worried about the matters of delay too much. Furthermore, I believe the government should take more efforts on infrastructure construction and ensure a better urban life for all of its citizens.

高分词汇

severe car crash 严重汽车碰撞
could not sense 感觉不了
ahead of schedule 比预期计划提前
miserable halt 令人痛苦的堵塞
zoomed 高速前进

为什么是 6 分?

Coherence(6 分)	Lexical Resource (7 分)	Grammar Range and Structure (7 分)
✓ 使用多种局内和句子的连接;条理比较清晰。 × 回答的最后部分有偏题的嫌疑;可能导致轻微扣分。 ✓ 回答长度可接受,能超过 1 分 30 秒的基本要求。	✓ 有使用和题目相关的专用名词和形容词。 ✓ 展示一定数量的"接地气"词汇;答案比较口语化。 ✓ 有展示明显的同义替换。	✓ 有使用一定数量的数复杂句。 ✓ 大部分的句子和时态都正确。

高分答案

Well, to be honest, I've been through quite a few major traffic jams in my life, more than the fingers I have on my hands really. But if I had to choose a particular traffic jam I think I would have to talk about the time when I was nearly late for my high school exams.

I was taking the bus, like what I always do every day to get to school, and because it was in the morning, I decided to take a quick snooze before my stop. However, on that particular day, I was awoken by a nice symphony of horns and shouting. I didn't think it was anything special back then but it did feel quite weird with all the sudden commotion happening outside my window. I soon realised it wasn't a normal traffic jam when I suddenly heard a series of blues and twos rushing past the bus I was on. I instantly went "uh-oh" thinking something disastrous must have happened.

Being a nosy brat back then, I stuck my head outside the window to see what was happening. I was expecting some massive 7 or 8 cars pile-up but I was really pissed off when it was actually just two blokes going at each other in the middle of the bloody road! I couldn't really see what happened to their cars but I guess it was because one of them bumped into the other person. We ended up being stuck in a long line of traffic for the next half an hour or so and I was getting really frustrated because I was afraid of missing my exams.

The good thing was, the police managed to settle the dispute between the two stupid lads and I managed to arrive at my exam just in the brink of time.

高分词汇

like what I always do 像我平时一样
quick snooze 小睡
symphony of horns 各种鸣笛声
sudden commotion 突然之间的骚动
traffic jam 塞车;交通拥堵
blues and twos 警察车
pile-up 多车交通事故
bumped 碰撞
stuck in a long line of traffic 交通拥堵动不了
brink of time 刚刚准时

为什么高分?

Coherence(8 分)	Lexical Resource (8 分)	Grammar Range and Structure (8 分)
✓ 能适当展开话题,每段思路明显。 ✓ 能灵活和准确使用多元化的连接词和信号词。 ✓ 回答详细;能达到 2 分钟的最高要求。	✓ 使用了中高级词汇和多种地道的习语和俚语;回答非常地道。 ✓ 使用多种专用名词和相关的形容词来更准确地描述话题。 ✓ 多次出现同义替换。	✓ 多次使用复杂结构来准确展开话题和保持连贯性。 ✓ 没有明显的语法和时态错误,准确度极高。

Describe a journey that you remember well
you should say:
where you went
what you did at this place
and explain why you like this journey

题目思路和方向(idea brainstorm)

这是一个两层问题(2-tier question),所以必须找出这个 part 2 问题的**两个关键词组**才能满足考官对考生答案的要求。一起通过一些问题和有用的理念来热热身吧:

1. A journey：去哪里？路途中看到什么，遇到什么？可以用三句短句来描述一下？坐什么交通工具去？当时要去干吗？为什么会选这个交通工具？

2. Remember well：为什么记得那么清楚？当时有什么感受？路程完成后有什么感想？

6 分答案

I'd like to talk about a journey of mine by boat, which was a long-long-ago experience of mine. When I was a P2 student, we were once organized to tour the Shanghai Grand Garden, home of the Chinese classical novel, the Dream of Red Mansions. What was exciting was that we were going to go there by boat! Before that, I had travelled by boat. So, I felt quite excited.

On the day, we walked from our school to the landing dock. To my surprise, the boat looked so huge and beautiful because of the Chinese traditional style decorations. I couldn't wait to go aboard and found a good seat to have a good view of the scenery. There were a lot of people on the boat.

It was a sunny day. I felt a little sick at the beginning. But it was not long before I felt better. I saw the waves hitting the side of the boat and some birds flying over the river. There were many trees on both sides of the river. As we were approaching the destination, we saw lots of one-storey small houses along the banks. And then, I looked at the people on the boat. Some were chatting with others in a happy mood, some were reading books, magazines or newspapers, and others were staring at the river side. The scene was so mesmerizing which was just like a beautiful picture. It took about two hours for us to get to the Grand Garden. When it was time to go ashore, I felt sad to depart.

高分词汇

organized to tour 安排去游览
landing dock 上岸码头
go aboard 上船
go ashore 上岸
found a good seat 找到好的位子
depart 离开

为什么是 6 分？

Coherence（7 分）	Lexical Resource（6 分）	Grammar Range and Structure（6 分）
✓ 使用多种句子连接。 ✓ 总体回答比较有条理性；有逻辑性地展开。 ✓ 回答长度可接收，能超过 1 分 30 秒的基本要求。	✓ 有使用和题目相关的专用名词和形容词； × 但是偏向简单词。 ✓ 使用少量“接地气”词汇。 ✓ 有展示明显的同义替换。	✓ 有使用一定数量的数复杂句； × 但是当中有些不太地道的句型出现。 ✓ 大部分的句子和时态都正确。

高分答案

Right, I've been on a lot different trips before but I guess my most unforgettable journey would definitely be the time when I cycled across the United States. In the summer of 2010, I cycled coast-to-coast across the United States with two of my best buds from University.

The three of us met at the University of Exeter, and we shared an interest in cycling. We regularly went on biking and camping trips into the Dartmoor country park at weekends if we had time on our hands. During our final year, we decided that it would be a great idea to train up and attempt to cycle across the North American continent to raise money for a charitable cause. So in July 2010, after months of training and preparation, we flew across the Atlantic Ocean to begin the seven thousand kilometer journey across the US.

The journey was far more challenging than we thought it would be. Both our mental and physical limits were put to the test as we cycled across mountains, deserts and rivers, sometimes going days without seeing any other people. We had to carry a lot of heavy equipment on our bikes, and we camped almost every night. If we were passing through a large town then we would stay in a hotel, to get a good night's rest and most importantly, have a hot shower! But more often than not, we would camp in the wild and wash in rivers and waterfalls.

Overall, we cycled seven thousand kilometers in forty nine days, and raised over four thousand pounds for a children's cancer charity, which I think is an incredible achievement.

高分词汇

unforgettable 难忘的
best buds 最好的兄弟
shared an interest 共同兴趣
had time on our hands 有时间
train up 锻炼
far more challenging than we thought 比想象中困难
put to the test 使受试验
going days 好几天
good night's rest 一晚的好睡眠
incredible achievement 很棒的成就

为什么高分?

Coherence(7 分)	Lexical Resource (8 分)	Grammar Range and Structure (8 分)
✓ 能适当展开话题,每段思路明显。 ✓ 能灵活和准确使用多元化的连接词和信号词。 ✓ 一半答案描述了背景资料;可以添加这个路程的相关信息。 ✓ 回答详细;能达到 2 分钟的最高要求。	✓ 使用了中高级词汇和多种地道的习语和俚语;回答非常地道。 ✓ 使用多种专用名词和相关的形容词来更准确地描述话题。 ✓ 多次出现同义替换。	✓ 多次使用复杂结构来准确展开话题和保持连贯性。 ✓ 没有明显的语法和时态错误,准确度极高。

Module 3　Speech 的结构

有时，我们在回答问题时会用"让步转折"的表达方式（although/though/but/however/yet），下面以 but 为例。

我们知道，but 之后的内容才是说话者真正想要表达的意思。例如：

Describe a wedding you attended

Answer: Ok, well actually the last time I was invited to a wedding was about fifteen years ago, **but** I'd try my best to recall everything happened that day.

很明显，这句话的重点是说"我会尽量回忆那天发生的事"。

既然 but 之后的内容是重点，那么我们就要重读 but 及其后我们讲的内容，来表示强调。

Module 4　练习

TIPS：

如果笔记格式混乱，会对考生阅读笔记造成干扰。记笔记时，最好使用项目符号或空格空行来表明层级，显得层次清晰、一目了然。例如：

思路：

air-conditioner

stopped working

only hot air

no cold air

(I) couldn't figure out (what was wrong)

(I was) furious (cos it took almost) 5 hours (for the) repairman (to show up.)

(I was) frustrated (cos the living room was so) hot (and I kept) sweating

(I felt) terrible (cos I had to pay the repairman) a large sum of money

笔记：

air-conditioner

- stopped working
  - ☆ only hot air
  - ☆ no cold air
- (I) couldn't figure out (what was wrong)
- (I was) furious
  - ▷ (cos it took almost) 5 hours (for the) repairman (to show up.)
- (I was) frustrated
  - ▷ (cos the living room was so) hot (and I kept) sweating
- (I felt) terrible
  - ▷ (cos I had to pay the repairman) a large sum of money

◇ Now write your notes within 1 min and then give a speech about it. 计时练习！一分钟时间记笔记，两分钟时间陈述。

Practice 1

Describe a law about environment you would like to see in the future
You should say:
what the law would be about
how this law will take effects
why it is important to have this law
and what changes will happen because of this law

Notes:

Practice 2

Describe a common vehicle in your city that you often use
You should say:
what it is
how often you use it
how much it costs to travel in it
and explain why you often use it

Notes:

Practice 3

Describe a place near water that you enjoyed visiting.
You should say：
where this place was
what you did at this place
who you went there with
and explain why you liked this place.

Notes：

Practice 4

Describe a person who likes to travel by plane.
You should say：
who this person is
how you know this person
where this person travels to
and explain why this person likes to travel by plane

Notes:

Part 3 Discussion

Module 1 考题回顾

对于 Transportation 和 Environment 这 2 个话题，如果考生没有提前准备过、没有思考过相关的问题，是很难在临场发挥时有比较完善的思路的。所以，同学们在备考时要重点思考 Transportation 和 Environment 这 2 个话题，并总结一些观点。以下是 Part 3 部分，Transportation & Environment 话题中，考官常问的一些问题。

1. What are the advantages and disadvantages of public transportation?
2. What are the advantages to society of having more people using mass transportation?
3. Why do some people have to travel a long distance every day to go to work?
4. What are the advantages and disadvantages of living in the centre of a city and living in the suburbs of a city?
5. Do you ever discuss the topic of the environment with your friends?
6. What do you think is the most serious environmental problem in China?
7. What are the different kinds of environmental problems that exist right now?

第 6 题问了你认为中国最严重的环境问题有哪些？关于环境问题，你能想到哪些呢？如果平时对这个话题关注得比较少，那么在考试中就很难有思路。我们在备考中可以在外文网站输入关键词，搜索出一些有关环境问题的报道，在回答问题时就可以借鉴。

网站推荐：

www. washingtonpost. com

www. nytimes. com

◇ Read 5 *Major Current Environmental Problems* and write your own thoughts about this topic. 阅读《现今五大主要环境问题》，并写出你的观点。

http://www.bcdef.com/ Education

5 Major Current Environmental Problems

1 Pollution: Pollution of air, water and soil require millions of years to recoup. Industry and motor vehicle exhaust are the number one pollutants. Heavy metals, nitrates and plastic are toxins responsible for pollution. While water pollution is caused by oil spill, acid rain, urban runoff; air pollution is caused by various gases and toxins released by industries and factories and combustion of fossil fuels; soil pollution is majorly caused by industrial waste that deprives soil from essential nutrients.

2 Global Warming: Climate changes like global warming is the result of human practices like emission of Greenhouse gases. Global warming leads to rising temperatures of the oceans and the earth' surface causing melting of polar ice caps, rise in sea levels and also unnatural patterns of precipitation such as flash floods, excessive snow or desertification.

http://www.bcdef.com/ Education

3 Overpopulation: The population of the planet is reaching unsustainable levels as it faces shortage of resources like water, fuel and food. Population explosion in less developed and developing countries is straining the already scarce resources. Intensive agriculture practiced to produce food damages the environment through use of chemical fertilizer, pesticides and insecticides. Overpopulation is one of the crucial current environmental problem.

4 Natural Resource Depletion: Natural resource depletion is another crucial current environmental problems. Fossil fuel consumption results in emission of Greenhouse gases, which is responsible for global warming and climate change. Globally, people are taking efforts to shift to renewable sources of energy like solar, wind, biogas and geothermal energy. The cost of installing the infrastructure and maintaining these sources has plummeted in the recent years.

5 Waste Disposal: The over consumption of resources and creation of plastics are creating a global crisis of waste disposal. Developed countries are notorious for producing an excessive amount of waste or garbage and dumping their waste in the oceans and, less developed countries. Nuclear waste disposal has tremendous health hazards associated with it. Plastic, fast food, packaging and cheap electronic wastes threaten the well being of humans. Waste disposal is one of urgent current environmental problem.

Module 2 Debate & Discussion

Debate: Work in two teams and debate. You have two minutes to think about what you are going to say. 分 2 组，围绕以下话题，进行辩论。（准备时间：2 分钟）

What are the advantages and disadvantages of private transportation?

Team A	Team B
Opinion 1 ________	Opinion 1 ________

Opinion 2 ____________ Opinion 2 ____________

Opinion 3 ____________ Opinion 3 ____________

Discussion: Discuss and answer the question below. 讨论以下话题。

Whose fault is it that we have these environment problems?

Part 4 Language Use

Module 1 语法改错

1. Why you think this?
2. I am not agree with her idea.
3. They been here for three years.
4. If the children are sick, they must to stay home and rest.
5. He just managed to avoid to hit the car in front of him.

Module 2 语音练习

Direction: cross the letters that you don't need to pronounce. 将不发音的字母划掉。

Example: The girl in the red coat was on a black bike just now.

1. We're going to work on a farm next Tuesday.
2. I bought a cheap book, but it's a good book.
3. — Do you know his bike number?
   — Sorry, I don't know.
4. The big bus from the factory is full of people.
5. What would you like, hot tea or black coffee?
6. I went there alone at nine last night.
7. It's a very cold day, but it's a good day.

Chapter 7 Hometown & Travel

话题词汇热身训练

Module 1 词汇

◇ Exercise 1. Make the following into sentences and read the sentences aloud. 用下列单词组成句子并大声朗读。

n.	*v.*	*adj.*
compound	immigrate	well-decorated
chandelier	chill out	rural
cost of living	ensure	zoological
unban lifestyle	mop the floor	botanical
package tour	swept	westernized
cultural shock	give a hand to	bright
washing machine	represent	tidy
sheet	improve	messy
furniture	fill my imagination with	responsible
shopping mall	rush to	educational
department store	end up	unknown
luxury shop	appeal to	romantic
boutique shop	soak up	meaningful
city hall	enrich one's knowledge	independswt
inhabitant	feast on	scenic
legend		famous
		refreshed
		sleepless

1. My hometown/a small-sized coastal city/the north of China/therefore/people/a slow-paced life/enjoy/seafood.

2. They/give/hand/visitors/in need/make/feel/at home.

3. It/been/my dream/go travelling/in Italy/enjoy the breathtaking view/Venice.

4. The apartment/I/in now/locate/the city center/a bunch of/cool diners and convenient shops/nearby.

5. The place/well-decorated/with/paintings/hang on the walls/amazing chandeliers.

◇ Exercise 2. Write down some words or phrases that you can think of within 30 seconds to answer these questions. And then work in pairs to ask and answer these questions. 流利度达成——30 秒内写出你能想到的可以回答下列问题的单词或词组！并与你身边的同学两人一组互相提问回答这些问题。

1. What are the main places of interest in your hometown? Why?

2. Do you like traveling?

3. Is your country large?

4. Can you describe the place where you live?

5. What are the requirements for your house decorations?

直 击 考 点

Module 1 Connectives 连接词 递进

◇ Underline the connectives in the following sentences and replace them with the words and phrases in the box. 划出下列例句中的连接词，并用方框里的连接词做替换练习。

another thing is	besides	. . . , as well	at the same time

1. Perth is famous for its unique landscape. In addition, it has the finest harbor in west Australia.

2. Doing housework always drives me crazy, plus I don't really live in the house that often anymore, which makes me feel even more useless wiping and cleaning stuff.

3. Every visitor enjoys the tropical view in my hometown, what's more the coastal activities like beach volleyball are really attracting for young people.

Module 2 Paraphrase 词群同义转换

◇ Write down the synonyms of the following words and describe the word to your group members. 写出下列单词的同义词，并用自己话向身边的同学描述这个单词。

Example: trip: tour, journey , voyage

✓ travel to another place

beautiful（形容地点）: ______________________

____

adapt: ______________________

____

amazing: ______________________

____

familiar: ______________________

____

Part 1 Interview

Module 1 Describe 描述

在雅思口语考试中，描述的能力一直是考察的重点之一。一方面在 Part 2 的话题卡部分，考官就会根据考生描述一个话题的内容以及表达来判断考生的语言能力。然而描述的考题在 Part 1 中其实也会出现，比如以下的题目：

- What's your hometown like?
- How's the weather in your hometown in summer?
- What does your favorite city look like?
- How do you like your hometown?
- Can you introduce your hometown a little bit?

在 Part 1 中，考生虽然不需要像 Part 2 的即兴演讲那样，进行全民描述，但是也应该做到有细节以及描述，切忌不可泛泛而谈，只给几个形容词就结束了，这样的回答是不具备 willing to speak at length 这个特征的，因此无法拿到 6 分以上的分数。

例如：What's your hometown like?

— My hometown is a small city. It's very clean and beautiful.

我们在回答的时候对于自己的这个描述要进行进一步的解释或者距离，考生不妨考虑以下几个方面。

1. State the most striking feature 形容令人印象深刻的特征

My hometown is **incredibly** interesting and full of historical sites.

My city is **definitely** the most picturesque in the whole country.

The city that I come from is not that big but terribly congested.

当然,你也不见得只能一味地夸赞你的家乡,有的时候反向的否定答案也会比较有新意

2. Introduce some of your personal experiences 谈一谈你自己的经验经历

Based on my own experience, I have never been to such a clean city that you can never find any rubbish or stuff like that along the streets.

One of my most unforgettable experiences was when I went to Seoul, there must be at least one coffee shop between every block. It's amazing.

If I remember rightly, the only place for sight-seeing or say relaxing is the forest park, which is quite far away from city center. And the whole class went to picnic there once in my high school.

◇ Exercise. Answer the following questions. 回答下列问题。

1. Can you describe the place where you live?

2. What does your favorite city look like?

3. Please describe the room you live in.

Discourse Markers

有一些雅思口语考题是有“限定对象”的。

例如: What kind of music do young people like? 这道题的限定对象就是 young people。请对比以下 2 个版本的 Answer:

Answer 1: ... Young people like pop music best ...

Answer 2: ... Unlike old people, young people like pop music best ...

我们可以看到, Answer 2 明显比 Answer 1 更有说服力,因为 Answer 2 将 old people 与 young people 做了对比,重点说明了“这是 young people 喜欢的音乐,而不是 old people 或其他群体喜欢的音乐”,通过对比,更加突出了 young people 这个群体在对于 music 的喜好。

在回答有“限定对象”的问题时,我们可以将“限定对象”与其他群体进行对比,来突出“限定对象”的特点。这时,我们可以使用一些表示对比与比较的 discourse markers, 例如:

Unlike ...

Compared with ...

Module 2 实战演练

➢ Examiner: Do you like your hometown?

Without saying. Hometown is the place where I was born and raised. Sure it's the most important place to me. Plus, my hometown is a nice small city with lovely natural landscape. For example, there is a small lake in the city center and several hills and parks.

➢ Examiner: What kind of museum do you like? Why?

I guess among all the museums that I have been to, art gallery is the one, coz honestly historical museums are kind of lame and scientific ones are more educational but not relaxing. However, art galleries are informative and give me a sense of beauty. What's more, there is normally a nice café within art galleries, which is my favorite place to chill out.

➢ Examiner: Do you use a map?

Sure. I use maps on my mobile phone every day. Frankly I'm terrible with directions. I get easily confused by those guideboards and stuff. I guess every one relies on maps and can't live without GPS nowadays.

➢ Examiner: What kind of housing/accommodation do you live in?

I live in an en-suite room in a duplex house. It belongs to a student accommodation company listed on my uni website. When I was trying to book a room on campus there was none. That's why I turned to those off campus. And this one is nearby the bus stop so it's not too bad.

➢ Examiner: Do you usually do any housework?

Sometimes. It really depends on my mood. Either way though it has to get done. Usually I pick up one house chore on Saturday, like scrubbing the toilet. And I had to do the dishes, make my bed, vacuum, and sometimes hand wash clothes.

➢ Examiner: What is special or unique about your country?

The first thing comes into my mind is panda. As we all know, panda is China's national treasure. China is the home to pandas and normally they live in some mountain areas in the west of China. I've seen them once in a natural park in Xi'an. They are super cute and lazy.

➢ Examiner: Where have you traveled to lately?

I traveled to Seoul with my bestie in May. It was a wonderful experience since my bestie and I share many things in common like tasting for food. And as we all know Seoul is the so-called shopping destination in Asia. I have to say we had a wonderful three day holiday there.

Module 3 练习

1. Is the place you are living good for your child? Why?

2. How long have you lived in your hometown?

3. Can you tell me about some famous landscapes in your hometown?

4. What are the people like in your hometown?

5. What kind of museum is more popular in china?

6. How much should we pay to go to museum?

7. Do you prefer to use electronic maps or those made of paper?

8. Do you know your neighbors? If not, Why?

9. What housework do you least like doing?

10. If you could change one thing about your country, what would it be?

11. Do you send postcards?

12. Have you ever sent postcards to others?

Part 2 The Long-turn

Module 1 Brainstorming 头脑风暴

◇ Read the examples of a brainstorming exercise. 请看以下头脑风暴的例子。

Dartmoor national park

- windy and cold
- wild
- moorland
- rock and stones
- remarkably beautiful
- plant
- cliffs

islan

- a little island
- in the Pacific
- peace and quite
- get away
- think clearly
- get a clear break
- self-change
- walk on the beach
- sit under the tree
- read books
- listen to the music go meet people

◇ Write down some words or phrases that you can think of to describe the topic given in the center. 脑洞大开，关于以下中心关键词，你能想到从哪些方面描述它，写下来吧。

a park I visited and

- feed the pigeons

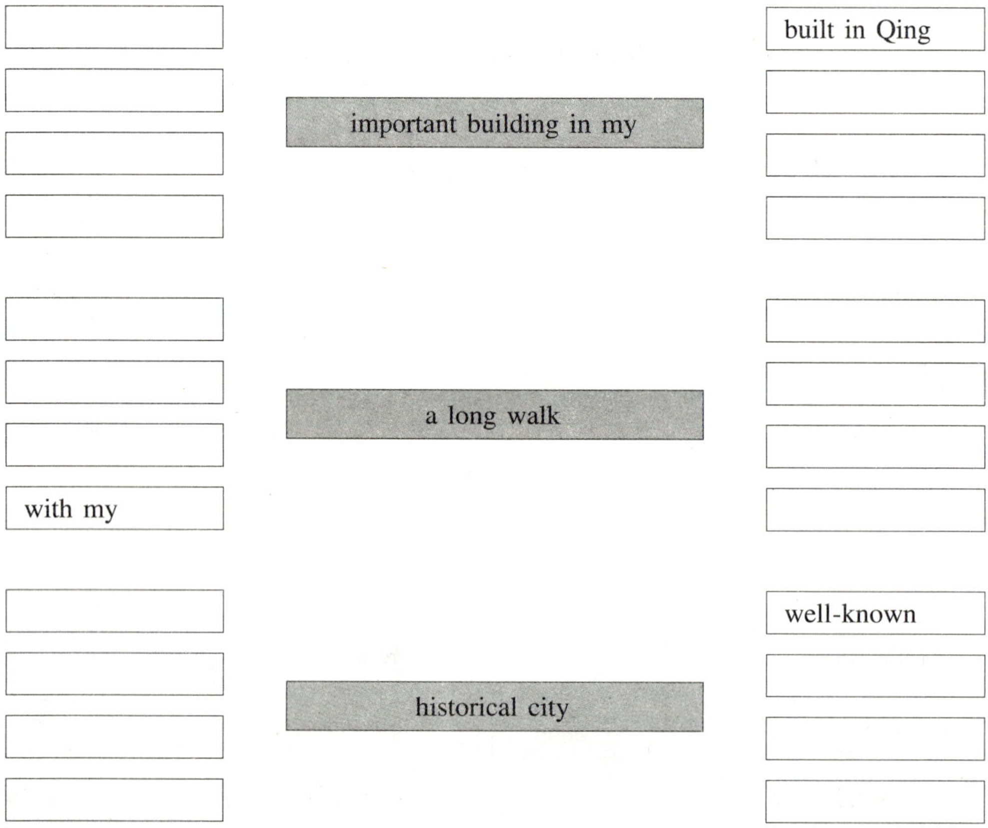

Module 2 实战演练

Describe your favourite part of your city (town)
You should say:
where it is
how you get there
what it looks like
and explain why you like it

题目思路和方向(idea brainstorm)

这是一个两层问题(2-tier question),所以必须找出这个 part 2 问题的**两个关键词组**才能满足考官对考生答案的要求。一起通过一些问题和有用的理念来热热身吧:

1. Part of the city:是什么地方?在你城市的什么地方?怎么去?方便去吗?可以描述一下吗?

a) Park/Garden — Lung of the city; greenery, sense of peace and quiet; small getaway; flora and fauna

b) Tourist attractions — busy; full of life; lots to see; take pictures; hustle and bustle;

historical importance.

c) Residential area — suburbs; inner city; community; sense of harmony; local culture; way of life.

d) Industrial zone — energetic; lots happening; range of noises; big and small factories

2. Favourite：为什么是最喜欢？最吸引你什么？在这个地方可以做什么？和谁一起去？

6 分答案

Today I want to talk about my favourite part of the city and this place is called Nanjing Road. It is located in the heart of the city center within the Huangpu district which is the busiest district in Shanghai and also home to the famous People Square Garden. Besides this, it is also very convenient to get to Nanjing road. You can get there by taking various forms of public transport such as the bus, taxi, and the underground which is only five minutes' walk from the place.

I guess there are several reasons why this place is my favourite part of my city. First of all, the scenery is really amazing. When you arrive at the road, you can see lines of different colored neon light signs which flicker in different ways depending on the design. I originally come from a small city so it is very rare to see so many big neon light signs in one place. Furthermore, Nanjing road is famous for its shopping as you can find many different shops there for example different branded shops that sell sportswear as well as shops that sell local food products such as pork jerkies. Whenever I go shopping in this city, I always think of Nanjing road and I always have a good time there.

高分词汇

heart of the city 城市的心脏地带
busiest 最繁忙的
various forms 不同种类
lines of 一排一排
flicker 一闪一闪
branded shops 名牌店

为什么是 6 分?

Coherence（7 分）	Lexical Resource（6 分）	Grammar Range and Structure（7 分）
✓ 使用多种局内和句子的连接+标志性词汇；条理比较清晰。 × 回答比较短，有可能不能说到 1 分 30 秒的基本要求。	✓ 有使用和题目相关的专用名词和形容词。 × 但是偏简单。 ✓ 使用了少量“接地气”词汇。 × 但是还是偏向写作的回答。 ✓ 有展示明显的同义替换。	✓ 有使用一定数量的复杂句。 ✓ 大部分的句子和时态都正确。

高分答案

There are lots of places I like to go, depending on my mood. Today though, I'm going to tell you about a special place near to where I live. I will explain where it is and how I get there. I will try and describe what it looks like and explain why I like the location so much.

I am lucky, although I live in a city, from my house I can walk to the edges of the Dartmoor national park, which is just a few miles from the city centre. To get to the national park I have to walk from my house down some local roads, and up a steep hill past some derelict houses. Dartmoor national park can be a really wild place, with its vast expanses of open moorland. You are high up, and it is quite exposed so it can be very windy and cold even in the summer. There are rocky outcrops and strange configurations of stones that have been weathered by centuries of wind and rain to create dramatic shapes. Some boulders are in piles, and there are steep vertical cliffs too.

The area attracts lots of people who like walking, climbing and bouldering because of its unique and beautiful landscape. Everywhere is dark wet peat under foot, and lots of heather. This is a low growing plant that flowers at the end of the summer turning the whole landscape purple. The park covers a huge area, I think around five hundred square miles, so the terrain differs from area to area, of course I am biased, but I believe I live near the most remarkably beautiful part of my city.

高分词汇

edges of ……的周边
really wild place 荒野的地方
vast expanses 广大无边的空间
quite exposed 蛮暴露的
rocky outcrops 露出地面的岩层
strange configurations of stones 奇怪的石头排列
weathered 风化的
dramatic shapes 有趣的形状
bouldering 攀爬石头
remarkably 非常的

为什么高分?

Coherence(8 分)	Lexical Resource (8 分)	Grammar Range and Structure (8 分)
✓ 能适当展开话题,每段思路明显。 ✓ 能灵活和准确使用多元化的连接词和信号词。 ✓ 回答详细;能达到 2 分钟的最高要求。	✓ 使用了中高级词汇和多种地道的习语和俚语;回答非常地道。 ✓ 使用多种专用名词和相关的形容词来更准确地描述话题。 ✓ 多次出现同义替换。	✓ 多次使用复杂结构来准确展开话题和保持连贯性。 ✓ 没有明显的语法和时态错误,准确度极高。

> Describe a place you would go if you were given the chance to travel anywhere in the world.
>
> You should say:
> where the place is
> what you would like to do there
> and explain why you would like to visit this particular place

题目思路和方向(idea brainstorm)

这是一个两层问题(2-tier question),所以必须找出这个 part 2 问题的**两个关键词组**才能满足考官对考生答案的要求。一起通过一些问题和有用的理念来热热身吧:

1. Place + anywhere in the world:是什么地方?在地球上的什么位子?怎么去?方便去吗?可以描述一下吗?

2. If you were given the chance:为什么有机会才去?背后的故事是什么?为什么特别想去这个地方?去了之后会有什么改变?

关于旅行的一些思路和词汇:

a) Arrangements — End of semester, need a holiday, each day's activity, printed on the blue sheet; information guides, explorer trip, have a different focus.

b) Activities — go camping, go the park or beach, hire boats, go boating, scuba diving, horse riding, watch underwater life, raise domestic animals, rocky bluffs, animals and birds, sea creatures, spectacular views, picnic and barbecue.

c) Equipment — van, a sleeping bag, bathers, good hiking boots and socks, warm sweater, jacket for the evenings, booking beds in a youth hostel.

d) Feelings — have a great stay, feeling relaxed and refreshed, no newspaper or television, "get away from it all" experience, unwind and appreciate the world, without a lot of interruption and distractions, cabin balcony, sit on our balcony, relax and unwind and enjoy the views, the rainforest wildlife, the only noise you should hear is the birds, discover something new in the rainforest.

6 分答案

So, let me describe to you a place I would like to go if I were given a chance to and this place is Ecuador. It is a small country located in the Central America This country becomes known to me because of a blog from the internet which is titled, "Ten countries you must visit before thirty" when I was searching for some information about a presentation. Whilst looking at this website, I found many fascinating facts about this country which made me want to visit this country.

So, in Ecuador, the official language is Spanish and ninety percent of the population is mixed raced meaning they have ancestors that come from different countries. Also, the views there are exquisite and fantastic because the country has beautiful coastlines and beaches.

Ecuador is the country I want to visit most mainly because there is an amusing tradition of giving names to people. They can name children after whatever they like, such as eleven rabbits, the mouse of snakes, and smoke. Some even name their children after famous celebrities like Clinton and Reagan. Another special thing about this country that attracts me is its strange weather. You know, Ecuador is a besides the sea which means it experiences frequent hurricanes and tornadoes. As a result of these extreme weather features, it will bring fish from the sea and scatter them from the air. I figure this is really an interesting country and given the time and money, I'd like to visit it in the near future.

高分词汇

fascinating facts 有趣的数据
mixed raced 混血
exquisite 优美的
beautiful coastlines and beaches 漂亮的海岸线和沙滩
amusing tradition 有趣的传统
given the time and money 如果我有时间和金钱的话

为什么是 6 分?

Coherence(7 分)	Lexical Resource (6 分)	Grammar Range and Structure (6 分)
✓ 使用多种局内和句子的连接;条理清晰。 × 思维有点跳跃;没有把描述和回答者的自身情况结合。 ✓ 回答长度可接受,能超过 1 分 30 秒的基本要求。	✓ 有使用和题目相关的专用名词和形容词;有些比较高级。 ✓ 使用了少量“接地气”词汇。 ✓ 有展示明显的同义替换。	✓ 有使用不同的简单句型和复杂句。 ✓ 大部分的句子和时态都正确。 × 但是出现一下明显的语法错误。

高分答案

If I could go somewhere of my choice, I would choose a little island in the Pacific Ocean. I could get away from my usual environment and influences so as to think clearly about what I want to do with my life. In spite of what others might think about me, I know I am not running away from something but to something. I want to get a clear break.

So once settled into my room on the little island of the Pacific Ocean, I could begin my process of self-change. I really could be anywhere as long as nobody could reach me by phone and I could have the peace and quiet to think about what I want to do. I would spend the mornings going for long walks on the beach and the afternoons sitting under my favourite tree, reading books and listening to all kinds of music. Probably most important of all, I would force myself to get out of my room and go to meet people.

I'm actually quite shy; but I might decide it's time for me to become someone who could be perfectly capable of having a conversation with anyone I choose. Since nobody would know the "real" me, the way I have always been, I might feel free to be completely different. I would push myself to experiment with the new ways of being. I would sample alternative lifestyles and pretend to be a different person. I would act in unfamiliar ways just to see how it felt.

高分词汇

clear break 绝对放松的休息
self-change 自我改变
reach me 联系我
peace and quiet 清静和安静
force myself 强迫自己
perfectly capable 绝对有能力
push myself 超越自我
experiment 尝试
alternative lifestyles 不一样的生活方式
unfamiliar ways 没接触过的方式

为什么高分?

Coherence(7 分)	Lexical Resource (8 分)	Grammar Range and Structure (8 分)
✓ 能适当展开话题,每段思路明显。 ✓ 能灵活和准确使用多元化的连接词和信号词。 ✓ 回答详细。 × 但是偏短,某些观点可以再扩展一些。	✓ 使用了中高级词汇和多种地道的习语和俚语;回答非常地道。 ✓ 使用多种专用名词和相关的形容词来更准确地描述话题。 ✓ 多次出现同义替换。	✓ 多次使用复杂结构来准确展开话题和保持连贯性。 ✓ 没有明显的语法和时态错误,准确度极高。

Module 3 Speech 的结构

在回答问题时,我们会用到 not only ..., but also ... (不仅……,而且……)这个结构来表示递进。很明显,but also 后面才是最主要的内容,not only 后面是相对次要的内容。例如:

Describe a job you would like to do in the future

Answer: I'd like to be a surgeon in the future ... Not only are surgeons well-paid, but also their contributions are highly appreciated ...

在这段答案中,这名考生想要成为一名外科医生的最主要的理由是 their contributions are highly appreciated。

我们应该重读 but also 及其后的内容 their contributions are highly appreciated 来表示强调。

Module 4 练习

TIPS：

请比较一下两个笔记的例子。

Note 1

My computer stopped working.

I couldn't solve the problem.

I called the repairman.

The repairman fixed the computer.

The repairman changed me a big sum of money.

Note 2

My computer	stopped working	
I	couldn't solve	the problem
I	called	the repairman
The repairman	fixed	the computer
The repairman	changed	me a big sum of money

建议同学们按照 Note 2 的形式记笔记，这样每句话的主、谓、宾就可以一目了然了。

◇ Now write your notes within 1 min and then give a speech about it. 计时练习！一分钟时间记笔记，两分钟时间陈述。

Practice 1

Describe a short journey that you disliked.

you should say：

where you went

who you went with

what you did and explain why you disliked this journey

Notes：

Practice 2

Describe a foreign country you want to visit but haven't been to.
You should say:
where this place is
what it is like
what you can do in this country
and explain why you want to visit the country.

Notes:

Practice 3

Describe a museum or library that you visited.
You should say:
where it was
what it looked it
what facilities it had
and explain what influence it had on you

Notes:

Practice 4

> Describe an important building in your hometown.
> You should say:
> where it is
> what it looks like
> what it is used for
> and explain why it is important.

Notes:

Part 3 Discussion

Module 1 考题回顾

Hometown 和 Travel 这 2 个话题看似很简单，但在 Part 3 部分，考官会根据这 2 个话题问一些比较有深度的问题，这样就会提高问题的难度，因此同学们在备考时还是要提前准备一些思路的，避免在考场上无话可说的情况。以下是 Part 3 部分，Hometown & Travel 话题中，考官常问的一些问题。

1. What is the difference between your hometown and other cities?
2. What are the advantages to society of having more people using mass transportation?
3. What places should foreigners visit in your hometown? Why?
4. Why do people need to travel every day?
5. What problems can people have when they are on their daily journey, for example to work or school? Why is this?
6. How long do you think is a suitable time for a holiday to be?
7. Are there some areas in your country where tourism is having a negative effect?

第 7 题问了旅游业的负面影响。在回答这个问题时，我们不妨从对经济的影响、对社会的影响以及对环境的影响三个方面下手。我们在备考中，也可以在外文网站输入关键词，搜索出一些有关旅游业负面影响的报道，在回答问题时就可以借鉴。

网站推荐：

www. news. bbc. co. uk

www. pulitzer. org

◇ Read *Negative Effects of Tourism* and write your own thoughts about this topic. 阅读《旅游业的负面影响》，并写出你的观点。

http://www.bcdef.com/ Education

Negative Effects of Tourism

Economic Effects

Successful tourism relies on establishing a basic infrastructure, such as roads, visitor centers and hotels. The cost of this usually falls on the government, so it has to come out of tax revenues. Jobs created by tourism are often seasonal and poorly paid, yet tourism can push up local property prices and the cost of goods and services. Money generated by tourism does not always benefit the local community, as some of it leaks out to huge international companies, such as hotel chains. Destinations dependent on tourism can be adversely affected by events such as terrorism, natural disasters and economic recession.

http://www.bcdef.com/ Education

Social Effects -- Negative

Visitor behavior can have a detrimental effect on the quality of life of the host community. For example, crowding and congestion, drugs and alcohol problems, prostitution and increased crime levels can occur. Tourism can even infringe on human rights, with locals being displaced from their land to make way for new hotels or barred from beaches. Interaction with tourists can also lead to an erosion of traditional cultures and values.

Environmental Effects -- Negative

Tourism poses a threat to a region's natural and cultural resources, such as water supply, beaches, coral reefs and heritage sites, through overuse. It also causes increased pollution through traffic emissions, littering, increased sewage production and noise.

Module 2 Debate & Discussion

Debate: Work in two teams and debate. You have two minutes to think about what you are going to say. 分2组，围绕以下话题，进行辩论。（准备时间：2分钟）

What are the advantages and disadvantages of travelling alone?

Team A	Team B
Opinion 1 ______________	Opinion 1 ______________
Opinion 2 ______________	Opinion 2 ______________
Opinion 3 ______________	Opinion 3 ______________

Discussion: Discuss and answer the question below. 讨论以下话题。

What can you learn from travelling abroad?

Part 4 Language Use

Module 1 语法改错

1. We've spent about $500 to buy food for the party.
2. I look forward to hear your reply soon.
3. New students often feel shy to talk to foreign teachers.
4. We're not allowed to skateboarding in the park.
5. He lost the race because he had to stop tying his shoelace.

Module 2 语音练习

Direction: mark the words with the pronunciation rule you leaned today. 划出具有同化发音规则的单词并朗读以下句子。

1. It's raining cats and dogs.
2. He stopped reading and looked up.
3. "On my way home, I looked up an old friend of mine."
4. He pulled a tired smile when he stepped out of the room.
5. Before I eat dinner, I read the newspaper for a while.
6. We read the newspaper every morning.
7. A: He is not the man he used to be.
8. B: Don't worry. You'll get used to it in no time.
9. We used to go there every year.
10. Our company used to do business with theirs.

Chapter 8 Food & Culture

话题词汇热身训练

Module 1 词汇

◇ Exercise 1. Make the following into sentences and read the sentences aloud. 用下列单词组成句子并大声朗读。

n.	*v.*	*adj.*
burger	boil	tasty
biscuits	bake	raw
chips	stew	nutritious
fries	chop	greasy
celery	celebrate	junk
cabbage	cut my budget on sth.	disgusting
cheese	resist	salty
sneakers	consume	sour
high-heels	have a good appetite	bitter
handbag	be passionate about	rich
shoulder bag	get tired of	on sale
clutch	honor	timesaving
tote	serve	economical
dragon boat festival	worry about	reasonable
high calories	release hunger	refreshing

1. She/taking exercises/lose weight/from day to day.

2. Chinese children/like/buy many firecrackers/the Spring Festival.

3. I'm/consider/buy/a second-hand computer/I/short/money now.

4. In my opinion/ability/painting/depend/mainly/talents.

5. I believe/it's/young/are/passionate about celebrating Christmas/than/old are.

◇ Exercise 2. Write down some words or phrases that you can think of within 30 seconds to answer these questions. And then work in pairs to ask and answer these questions. 流利度达成——30 秒内写出你能想到的可以回答下列问题的单词或词组！并与你身边的同学两人一组互相提问回答这些问题。

1. Do you like shopping?

2. What sort of clothes do you like to wear?

3. What do other people in your country usually do on public holiday?

4. Do you like to eat fruit(s) and vegetables?

5. What is your favourite snack?

直击考点

Module 1 Connectives 连接词 强调

Underline the connectives in the following sentences and replace them with the words and phrases in the box. 划出下列例句中的连接词，并用方框里的连接词做替换练习。

1. She was very fond of speaking French, which indeed she spoke well.
2. He will of course say yes to my proposal.
3. Most importantly, you must work hard to catch up.
4. I know, but I like canned fruit, especially canned pineapple.

surely	undoubtedly	the thing is	actually
in particular	absolutely		

Module 2 Paraphrase 词群同义转换

◇ Write down the synonyms of the following words and describe the word to your group members. 写出下列单词的同义词，并用自己话向身边的同学描述这个单词。

Example：delicious：tasty，mouth-watering，savory，appetizing

✓

restaurant：________________________________

____

unhealthy：________________________________

____

buy：________________________________

____

eat：________________________________

____

Part 1 Interview

Module 1 Ability：Are you good at doing sth.？

Are you good at cooking?

这个章节，我们讲来学习如何回答关于做某件事的能力的 Part 1 考题。首先，我们会发现，这些句子是我们之前学过的一般疑问句。也就是说在回答时，需要先告诉考官是或否，然后再进一步展开。

在这类问题的展开部分，我们不妨就这个能力或者说技能的具体情况以及掌握或者没有掌握的原因进行扩展。

肯定的：

I'm able to do some simple housework.

I have a genius for cooking.

I have an eye for something.

否定的：

I'm terrible with something.

I do not know the first thing about doing something.

I don't know the first thing about something.

进一步解释：

The reason behind this is ... （原因是……）

The most influential fact is ... （最有影响的因素是……）

I'll give the credit to ... （这件事要归功于……）

◇ Exercise. Answer the following questions. 回答下列问题。

◇ Can you cook?

◇ Are you able to make a meal by yourself?

◇ Are you good at painting?

◇ How good are you at cooking?

◇ Do you know how to cook?

◇ Are you capable of cooking?

Module 2 实战演练

➢ Examiner: Do you like your name?

Well, kind of. I wouldn't say that I'm 100% satisfied with my name, coz honestly it's a very common name in China. I mean all the characters. My given name is xin which means happiness and promising in Chinese. I guess it's a hope given by my dad.

➢ Examiner: Do you ever receive letters or cards?

Yep. I got a friend who really enjoys sending postcards while traveling. No matter where she is, she'll pick a cute postcard and write a few words. I think it's kind of cool, coz every time I received the card I felt surprised and touched.

➢ Examiner: What types of bags do you use?

My favorite is definitely tote bag. It's a type of roomy bags and it just fits me perfectly. I don't know why it just seems like I have to carry everything with me. Otherwise I'll feel insecure. I guess it's a type of OCD, too.

➢ Examiner: Is food important to you?

Absolutely. I'm a foodie and I enjoy trying different types of food. And I think the most important thing is to keep a variety of diet, and that's why I try to eat both vegies and meat no matter I'm eating at home or dining out.

➢ Examiner: What kind of food do you particularly like?

My current fav is Vietnamese, like pho. It tastes like soup noodles but more addictive. I guess lime is the reason behind this. I'm really into the sour taste. You must try it if you've never tasted it before.

Module 3 练习

1. Are you willing to try some new food?

2. What do you consider to be a healthy diet?

3. Where do you usually buy clothes?

4. Do you prefer shopping alone or with others?

5. What is the difference between clothes that people wear on weekdays and weekends?

6. Have you ever been to a live concert?

7. What kinds of things do you like to draw?

8. Do people in your country celebrate Christmas?

9. Is it easy (or, convenient) for you to buy fruit and vegetables?

10. What kind of snack is popular in your country?

11. What kinds of shoes do you like?

Part 2 The Long-turn

Module 1 Brainstorming 头脑风暴

◇ Read the examples of a brainstorming exercise. 请看以下头脑风暴的例子。

cook steamed fish
step 1: get all the ingredients
step 2: place the fish on a shallow dish

step 3: drizzle a little soy sauce and water over the fish
step 4: scatter the ingredients evenly over the fish
step 5: place the fish on a rack in a wok
step 6: steam the fish for fifteen minutes
step 7: serve the dish

authentic food　　amazing design　　in the city center

a Caribbean restaurant

fresh aromas　　decorations　　nice dinner

◇ Write down some words or phrases that you can think of to describe the topic given in the center. 脑洞大开，关于以下中心关键词，你能想到从哪些方面描述它，写下来吧。

a traditional Chinese festival
step 1:
step 2:
step 3:
step 4:
step 5:
step 6:
step 7:

______　______　______

a song

______　singer　______

______　______　______

an interesting speech

______　______　lecturer

______　______　______

a show you enjoyed watching

______　______　performers

Module 2 实战演练

> Describe a special dish you ate
> You should say
> what you ate
> where you had this dish
> who you ate with
> and explain why this was a special dish

题目思路和方向(idea brainstorm)

这是一个两层问题(2-tier question),所以必须找出这个 Part 2 问题的**两个关键词组**才能满足考官对考生答案的要求。一起通过一些问题和有用的理念来热热身吧:

1. Special dish:是什么的食物?什么时候吃?和谁一起吃?通常在哪里吃?为什么觉得特别?这个菜怎么做的?

a) Beef — imported from Japan; the best you can find; helps to build our bodies; if you live in a cold climate you need a lot of fat.

b) Sichuan-style sausages — very spicy; good for home cooking or a picnic.

c) Star fruit — from a local organic farm; no chemical contamination; juicy; fresh and cheap.

2. You ate:为什么喜欢吃?味道如何?能描述一下这款菜吗?吃的时候有什么感受?

6 分答案

Today I want to describe a special dish I ate and this dish is called Chinese curry chicken rice. This is one of the most popular dish in my hometown and a lot of people eat it in the restaurants every day. The rice is first boiled in water and then the boiled rice is stir-fried with tender boneless chicken and fresh vegetables. The curry sauce is prepared separately using some herbs and spices and the chicken is added to the curry sauces at the end. The side dish salad is prepared using different green leafy vegetables like lettuces and fruits and those are cut into pieces which are then mixed together with mustard. All three items are served together.

I eat this dish approximately three to four times a week. This dish is usually prepared in local low end restaurants and that's why I only eat it when I'm out and about. There are multiple variations in the way this dish is prepared. Different restaurants have their own secret recipe for the curry and this is what makes it very special.

I love eating this dish for many reasons, firstly because it is very delicious and healthy. This meets the demand for different food requirement our body needs. Besides this, it is available in most parts of my hometown so it is very convenient to find. Last of all, it is not that expensive to buy so it doesn't leave my pocket empty.

高分词汇

stir-fried 炒
prepared 准备
served together 一起端上
variations 不同种类
secret recipe 秘密食谱
leave my pocket empty 不会让我破产

为什么是 6 分?

Coherence(6 分)	Lexical Resource (6 分)	Grammar Range and Structure (6 分)
✓ 使用一系列连接词。 × 但是无法保持回答连贯性。 ✓ 回答长度可接收,能超过 1 分 30 秒的基本要求。	✓ 有足够和针对性的词汇来回答问题。 × 但是有使用不当的地方。 × 某些词汇多次重复。 ✓ 展示少量"接地气"词汇。 × 但是同时也包含了写作应用词汇。 ✓ 有展示明显的同义替换。	✓ 有使用一定数量的复杂句。 ✓ 大部分的句子和时态都正确。 × 但是有些明显的错误。

高分答案

I am not much of a cook, but I do cook one dish well — steamed fish. It is my mom's specialty. When I moved out of my parents' house, I missed it so much that I asked mom to teach me how to cook it. And now I can make restaurant quality steamed fish.

Cooking steamed fish is super easy. But to get the most out of this recipe, make sure the fish you use is alive, or at least fresh. You also need gingers, spring onions, mushrooms and chili. First, clean the fish, cut the stalks of spring onions to almost two inch lengths, slice gingers and cut up mushrooms and chilies. Next, place the fish on a shallow dish and drizzle a little soy sauce and water over the fish. After that, scatter the rest of the ingredients evenly over the fish. Finally, place the dish on a rack in a wok with some water and steam it on high heat for ten to fifteen minutes. It is served hot and it is perfect in every way.

Steamed fish is a dish that the Chinese usually make on special occasions like Chinese New Year. I would usually prepare the steamed fish on birthdays, parties and festivals because my family and friends love it. Steaming is the "purest" way to cook fish to bring out the delicate sweet flavor of it. Plus, it is healthy. It sure can beat any junk food or crappy takeaways.

高分词汇

specialty 专长
restaurant quality 饭店的品质
fresh 新鲜
drizzle 加一点点
evenly 均匀的
rack 支架
"purest" 最纯正
crappy takeaways 糟糕/不健康的外卖

为什么高分?

Coherence(7 分)	Lexical Resource (7 分)	Grammar Range and Structure (7 分)
✓ 能适当展开话题,每段思路明显。 ✓ 能灵活和准确使用多元化的连接词和信号词。 ✓ 回答详细;能达到 2 分钟的最高要求。	✓ 使用了中高级词汇和多种地道的习语和俚语。 × 但是有些不准确。 ✓ 使用多种专用名词和相关的形容词来更准确地描述话题。 ✓ 多次出现同义替换。	✓ 多次使用复杂结构来准确展开话题和保持连贯性。 ✓ 没有明显的语法和时态错误,准确度极高。

> Describe a restaurant that impressed you a lot
> You should say:
> where the restaurant was
> when you went there
> who you went with
> and explain why it impressed you a lot

题目思路和方向(idea brainstorm)

这是一个两层问题(2-tier question),所以必须找出这个 Part 2 问题的**两个关键词组**才能满足考官对考生答案的要求。一起通过一些问题和有用的理念来热热身吧:

1. A restaurant:餐厅叫什么?在哪里?什么时候会去?上一次去是什么时候?为什么会去?怎么去?和谁去?

a) Fast food Chains/Take-away shops — menu above the counter; pay the person who serves you; take your food, sit down or take-away, no need to leave a tip

b) Coffee shop — sit at the counter or a table; don't need to wait for a waitress to show you where to sit; brings you coffee when you sit down; you pay at the cashier when you leave

c) Family restaurant — casual; shows you where to sit; waitress gives you a doggy bag to take your leftover food; add addition money to bill as a tip

d) Top class restaurant — make a reservation; arrive on time; taste the wine; get a bill at the end; tip the waiter.

2. Impressed you：为什么留下深刻的印象？在餐厅里面有什么好吃的？环境如何？服务人员如何？

6 分答案

Of all the restaurants I could tell you about, Fortune house restaurant is probably the one that I would like to talk about the most. I last visited the restaurant around three weeks ago because I wanted to introduce my Spanish teacher to some Chinese dishes.

Fortune house is pretty famous for its seafood dishes especially its steamed sea bass and salt and peppered squid. I always enjoy visiting this restaurant for a number for reasons. First of all, the food there is of good quality and well prepared. For instances, they only use fish that is caught on the day in their fish dishes. Secondly, the catering staffs are always welcoming and polite. They will advice you on any specials on offer and they are always quick on their feet if you need any assistance. Thirdly, the restaurant is always spotlessly clean. That's why I always invite my foreign friends whenever they want try Chinese food as they tend to be quick picky about cleanliness.

Finally, the restaurant is situated near the middle of the city centre which means I'm able to take my girlfriend after nightfall without fearing for our personal safety and the lack of transportation to get back home.

高分词汇

well prepared 准备的/煮得很好
caught on the day 当天吊上来的
welcoming 很亲切
advice you 建议你
spotlessly clean 非常干净
picky 好挑剔的

为什么是 6 分？

Coherence(6 分)	Lexical Resource (6 分)	Grammar Range and Structure (7 分)
× 连接词欠缺＋重复使用连接词;大部分句子都是简单句。 × 没有出现话语标记。 × 考生可能出现明显的卡可和停顿。 × 回答偏短,未必能超过 part 2 回答要求(至少 1 分 30 秒)。	✓ 有使用和题目相关的专用名词。 × 但是欠缺形容词导致描述点比较跳跃。 ✓ 展示少量“接地气”词汇。 × 但是同时也包含了写作应用词汇。 ✓ 有展示明显的同义替换。	✓ 使用了简单和复杂句型来回答问题。 ✓ 大部分的句子和时态都正确。

高分答案

Hmm ... I've been to a lot of restaurants before and I must say "turtle bay" in Southampton left me with the best impression. It's mainly a Caribbean restaurant serving a wide range of authentic Caribbean foods such as spiced chicken wings and fruit curry. It is also positioned smack bang in the middle of the city centre so I would often eat at this establishment if I had to go out for a nice dinner.

To be honest, there are a few things that put this restaurant above others. For starters, I still remember my first time going there, which was my girlfriend's birthday. As I stepped into the restaurant, I noticed the decorations and I was taken back by it, especially with all the real — life wooden and tree like structures. Furthermore, the food there was fantastic with fresh aromas floating all the around the place. I felt like I wasn't in U. K. anymore but that I flew to the islands themselves and really set foot into a local tropical restaurant.

I've gone off course a bit, but because it was my girlfriend's birthday, turtle bay was very kind and treated us to 2 wonderful cocktails to celebrate the event. Together with the amazing design, I would really suggest everyone to pay a visit whenever you are visiting the city.

高分词汇

best impression 最好的印象
authentic 真正的
smack bang in the middle 正中间
establishment 建立;企业
put this restaurant above others 比其他餐厅都好
taken back 吃惊
fresh aromas 香味
pay a visit 参观一下

为什么高分?

Coherence(8 分)	Lexical Resource (8 分)	Grammar Range and Structure (8 分)
✓ 能适当展开话题,每段思路明显。 ✓ 能灵活和准确使用多元化的连接词和信号词。 ✓ 回答详细;能达到 2 分钟的最高要求。	✓ 使用了中高级词汇和多种地道的习语和俚语;回答非常地道。 ✓ 使用多种的专用名词和相关的形容词来更准确地描述话题。 ✓ 多次出现同义替换。	✓ 多次使用复杂结构来准确展开话题和保持连贯性。 ✓ 没有明显的语法和时态错误,准确度极高。

Module 3　Speech 的结构

当我们想要说明一件事情的两个不同方面时,可以使用 On one hand, ... On the other hand, ... 这个结构。

例如：

Whether to leave Shanghai or not? It was a hard decision. On one hand, she loved her job in Shanghai and didn't want to quit it. On the other hand, she couldn't bear the high cost of living in this city any more.

Module 4 练习

TIPS：

本章我们介绍一些记笔记时可以使用的缩写。同学们在备考时要多加练习使用，以熟悉这些缩写，在考场上才能熟练使用。下面是一些常见的缩写的方法，同学们可以根据这些方法创造符合自己记忆习惯的缩写。

1. 利用发音，例如：

face to face = face 2 face　　before = B4

Where are you = Where r u

2. 省略元音字母，例如：

manage = mng　　year = yr

3. 只记前几个字母，例如：

important = imp　　government = gov　　cooperate = coop

◇ Now write your notes within 1 min and then give a speech about it. 计时练习！一分钟时间记笔记，两分钟时间陈述。

Practice 1

Describe a person you know who is good at cooking.
You should say:
who this person is
what is your relationship with this person
what kinds of food he or she cooks
and explain why you think this person is so good at cooking

Notes:

Practice 2

> Describe a (type of) foreign food that you would like to try.
> You should say:
> the name of this food
> where you can eat it (Or: what country it comes from)
> how you know about this food
> and explain why you would like to try it.

Notes:

Practice 3

> Describe a plant grown in your country.
> You should say:
> what the plant is
> where it is grown
> why you like or dislike it
> and explain why it is important to your country.

Notes:

Practice 4

> Describe a foreign culture that you are interested in.
> You should say:
> what this culture is
> what you know about this culture
> how you learned about this culture
> and explain why you feel this culture is interesting.

Notes:

Part 3 Discussion

Module 1 考题回顾

对于 Food 这个话题,同学们在备考时要多积累描述食物的形容词和短语。例如,表达“好吃”除了 delicious, tasty 之外,你还知道别的表达方式吗? Culture 这个话题比较抽象,同学们在答题时最好举具体的例子,这样答案才不会显得空洞。以下是 Part 3 部分, Food & Culture 话题中,考官常问的一些问题。

1. Are there many vegetarians in China?
2. Do you think advertising has an effect on what foods people eat?
3. Are there many restaurants near your home/school/university/work place?
4. What different types of restaurants are there in your hometown?
5. Does the food in the restaurant you just talked about taste different to western food?
6. How do people learn about other cultures?

7. What do you think is the best way to become familiar with another culture?

第 6 题和第 7 题都是有关于如何学习海外文化。我们在备考中，也可以在外文网站输入关键词，搜索出一些有关学习海外文化的内容，在回答问题时就可以借鉴。

网站推荐：

www. msnbc. com

www. wikipedia. com

◇ Read *How Can I Learn About Different Cultures* and write your own thoughts about this topic. 阅读《我应该如何学习海外文化》，并写出你的观点。

http://www.bcdef.com/ Education

How Can I Learn About Different Cultures?

One way is to read books written by authors from a particular culture.

For example, when a teacher wishes to expose her students to a different culture, she will often read them stories based on a culture's folklore. To learn about various tribes of Native Americans, she may read students books like The Rough Face Girl by Rafe Martin or The Windigo's Return: A North Woods Story by Douglas Wood and Greg Couch. She may invite Native American storytellers to visit the classroom so students can listen to authentic tales from that particular culture.

http://www.bcdef.com/ Education

A person can learn about different cultures if she samples authentic food from a specific cultural group.

Seek out restaurants that feature authentic food from a variety of countries. Whether a person wants to learn more about regions in Japan, the Middle East, Africa, or any other world culture, becoming familiar with its food is a giant step in the right direction. Food is an important part of different cultures and allows people to gain insight into a particular cultural group's way of life.

People who love to meet people in far-flung areas of the world may not be able to travel in person, **but they can always sign up for a pen pal.**

The Internet has made it possible for people to correspond with others from different countries just by logging on to the world wide web. Various websites offer pen pal services, offering to connect individuals with pen friends located around the world. Corresponding with people from other countries through email or snail mail is another useful way to become familiar with different cultures.

Module 2 Debate & Discussion

Debate: Work in two teams and debate. You have two minutes to think about what you are going to say. 分2组,围绕以下话题,进行辩论。(准备时间:2分钟)

Do you think the ways people learn about other cultures today are different to the ways people used to get knowledge decades ago?

Team A

Opinion 1 ______________________

Opinion 2 ______________________

Opinion 3 ______________________

Team B

Opinion 1 ______________________

Opinion 2 ______________________

Opinion 3 ______________________

Discussion: Discuss and answer the question below. 讨论以下话题。

What are some of the factors that make a restaurant a good one?

Part 4 Language Use

Module 1 语法改错

1. The woman apologized to stand on my foot.
2. The driver spent a lot of time looking at his car keys.
3. He will start his course on July.
4. In China, the standard for living is much better than in the past.
5. The data took from 1960 to 1996.

Module 2 语音练习

Direction: mark the words with the pronunciation rule you leaned today. 划出具有同化发音规则的单词并朗读以下句子。

Now look what a mess you've made.
Do you miss your family?
I shall miss you very much.
Take care that you don't spoil your new clothes.
A: I'm very glad to meet you.
B: It's a pleasure to meet you.
I'm sorry to tell that you've been dismissed.
Would you show me the bathroom, please?
Would you care to go for a walk with me?
Could you do me a favor?
Could you possibly give me a lift home?
She has traveled in northern countries.
The southern half of the country is a desert.
She says help only the worthy poor.
This book is worthy of being read (to be read).

Chapter 9 Abstract topics

本章总结了一些雅思口语考试中出现过的抽象类话题，这类考题出现的频率不高，但通常比较难，希望各位考生考前结合自己考试的情况备考，做好准备。

这些抽象的话题一般是生活中一些特殊的体验和感受，或者一些思想感情的讨论，其实离我们的生活并不遥远。大家注意回答时还是要给出具体的事例讲解或者举例。

Part 1 Interview

Module 1 实战演练

➢ Examiner: What natural sound(s) do you like (the most)?

I like the sound of the night air blowing with a cool breeze, coz it's really calming. I like the feeling when I'm on my way walking back home hearing this sound of leaves along the street.

➢ Examiner: Do you mind noises?

Sure. I can't take noises. For example, I once lived in an apartment with the subway train station right across the street, a fire station around the corner, and to top it all off there was a dance club on the bottom floor of my building. I lived for only one night and moved out again even it's so tiring moving in and out.

➢ Examiner: Are cities becoming noisier?

Definitely. Nowadays, many cities are noisier than ever before because of the advanced technology. In the amazing development in technology science, we can see the industries are building up everywhere. Plus there are some urban stuff that teenagers like to play, such as motor-racing at the night therefore people find it hard to fall asleep.

➢ Examiner: What kinds of animals as a pet do the people have in your country?

Normally they have dogs like people in any other country in the world. Unfortunately many families in China don't really treat their pet as a family member whether it's a dog or cat. They just treat them as a companion. So we often hear pets being dumped in news coverage.

➢ Examiner: Are flowers important in your culture?

Not that important I guess. Only on some special occasions people would buy flowers to send friends or something like birthday and anniversary. But I find that in western countries people have a habit of buying flowers to decorate their house and I think it's really romantic.

Module 2 练习

1. Do you think you are a polite person?

2. How do people in your culture show good manners towards others?

3. What toys did you play with when you were a child?

4. Is it easy to concentrate on things?

5. How do you organize/manage your time?

6. Are you good at memorizing things?

7. Have you ever forgotten something that is important?

8. How do you memorize things?

9. Who do you think can remember things easier? The old or the young?

10. Does your school have any quiet places for studying?

11. Do you think cities are suitable places for keeping a pet?

12. What sounds remind you of your childhood?

Part 2 The Long-turn

Module 1 Brainstorming 头脑风暴

◇ Read the examples of a brainstorming exercise. 请看以下头脑风暴的例子。

Dartmoor national park

- windy and cold
- wild
- moorland
- rock and stones
- remarkably beautiful
- plant
- cliffs

islan

- a little island
- in the Pacific Ocean
- peace and quite
- get away
- think clearly
- get a clear break
- self-change
- walk on the beach
- sit under the tree
- read books
- listen to the music
- go meet people

◇ Write down some words or phrases that you can think of to describe the topic given in the center. 脑洞大开,关于以下中心关键词,你能想到从哪些方面描述它,写下来吧。

a park I visited and liked

- feed the pigeons

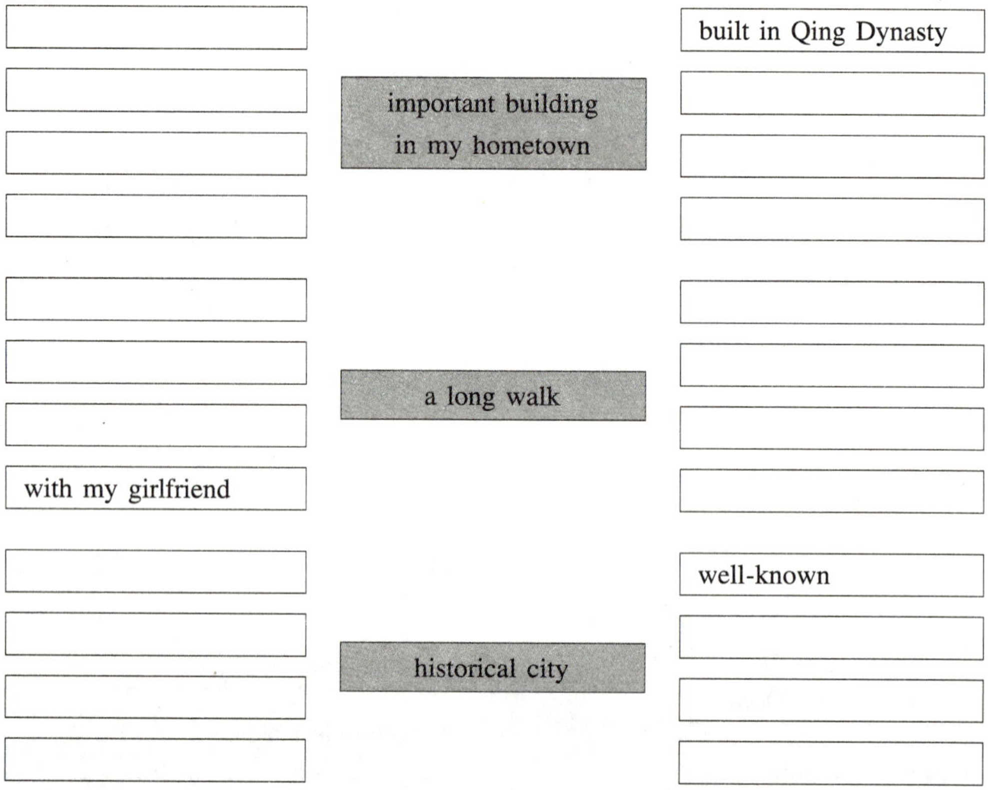

Module 2 实战演练

Describe a new skill you want to learn.
You should say
what it is
how you would learn it
where you can learn it
and explain why you want to learn it.

题目思路和方向(idea brainstorm)

这是一个两层问题(2-tier question)所以必需要找出这个 part 2 问题的两个关键词组才能慢满足考官对考生答案的要求。一起通过一些问题和有用的理念来热热身吧：

1. New skill：是什么技能？用来做什么？在哪里学习这个技能？如何学到这个技能？

2. You want to learn：为什么想要学？身边是否有人具有这个技能？过去有没有相关的经历？

a）Play the guitar-always wanted to learn a musical instrument since small；roommate；relatively easy

b）Swimming-breaststroke，lose weight，swimming training center

c) Skating-popular, trendy, indoor skating stadium

6 分答案

Speaking of a new skill that I wanna learn, final cut is the first thing that I came up with. I've been thinking about it for like at least two years. Final cut is a video cutting and editing software. Basically you can create your own movies and stuff. It's pretty cool. By adding a variety of effects between clips, a unique video will be done. Of course it's much more complex than I said. It's always easier said than done.

I first heard about it when I was seeing my roommate making a video for his parents wedding anniversary. He put some video clips he recorded in life and made them look like a movie. It was terrific. Oh and my favorite thing about it is you can choose music and songs you like as the background music. It's just awesome. And from then on I've been thinking about learning it. Last term I was about to have a chance to learn it, coz we had an optional course relating to video editing. But when I tried to pick it up, the course was no longer available.

I really want to learn it because I enjoy capturing every moment in my life, everything. I capture everything that is happening and people round me by my phone. Now the last thing I need is to make them more memorable and special. Next year, I guess I'll probably choose an online course or something. After all it's too complex to learn it by myself.

高分词汇

edit = 编辑
video clips = 视频短片
optional course = 选修课
pick up sth = 学会…
capture = 捕捉

为什么是6分?

Coherence(6分)	Lexical Resource (6分)	Grammar Range and Structure (6分)
✓ 使用一系列连接词。 × 但是无法保持回答连贯性,较为混乱。 ✓ 回答长度符合基本要求。	✓ 有足够和针对性的词汇来回答问题。 × 但是有使用不当的地方。 × 某些词汇多次重复。 × 同义替换较少。	✓ 有使用一定数量的复杂句。 ✓ 大部分的句子和时态都正确。 × 但是有些明显的错误。

Module 3 Speech 的结构

我们知道,雅思考试中有和 childhood 相关的话题,考生在描述自己小时候发生的事情时,可能由于时间久远,有些细节记不清了。这时,考生可以一开始就先告诉考官:"那是太

久之前发生的事”,“我不是很记得,但我会尽量回忆”,等等,然后再进行具体的描述。例如:

Describe a special toy you had in your childhood

You should say,

what it was

who gave it to you

how often you played it

and explain why it was special to you

Sample Answer:

I don't quite remember as it was quite some time ago. However, I still remember how it looked like so I'll focus that...

这样一来可以加长答案内容,二来使考生的回答显得更加真实,因为是小时候发生的事,所以记得不是很清楚是很正常的。

Module 4 练习

TIPS:

在上一章中,我们提到可以用缩写的方法来加快记笔记的速度。本章,我们介绍加快记笔记速度的另一个方法:使用符号。请看一下范例:

thrive/develop	↗
happy	☺
return	←
like	❤
at night	\
because	∵
so	∴
important	☆
with/and	&

同学们也可以在备考时创造一些符号来代替常用的一些词汇,并多加练习,这样才能在考试时熟练使用,加快记笔记的速度。

◇ Now write your notes within 1 min and then give a speech about it. 计时练习!一分钟时间记笔记,两分钟时间陈述。

Practice 1

Describe a museum or library that you visited.

you should say

where it was
what it looked like
what facilities it had
and explain what influence it had on you

Notes:

Practice 2

Describe the ideal flat or house that you would like to live in.
You should say
where it is
what you want to do there
what there are in the place
and explain why you want to live there

Notes:

Practice 3

Describe a foreign country you want to visit but haven't been to.
You should say:
where this place is
what it is like
what you can do in this country
and explain why you want to visit the country.

Notes:

Practice 4

> Describe a long journey you enjoyed
> you should say
> where you went
> when and why you went there
> what landscape you saw
> and explain why this was such an unforgettable trip

Notes:

Part 3 Discussion

Module 1 考题回顾

在 Part 3 部分，考生可能会被问到个人的经验（例如：第 1，2，3 题），也可能会被问到对某一个社会现象的看法（例如：第 4，5，6，7 题），同学们在备考时就要有所准备。

对于 Abstract 抽象类的话题，一定要给出具体的例子或者进行具体的解释，不能泛泛而谈。抽象类话题也是 Part 3 部分比较难的话题，想要冲击高分的同学一定要对这类话题有所准备。以下是 Part3 部分，Abstract 抽象类话题中，考官常问的一些问题。

1. Are you good at managing your time?

2. How do you manage your time?
3. When is it most important for you to manage your time?
4. What's the difference between dream and goal?
5. Compare the sleeping habits of young people and old people in your country.
6. Do you think it is necessary to create a law?
7. In your country's culture, how do you show that you are being polite?

第1,2,3题都问了与Time Management时间管理相关的问题。我们在备考中可以在外文网站输入关键词,搜索出一些有关时间管理的文章,在回答问题时就可以借鉴。

网站推荐:

www.edition.cnn.com

www.reference.com

◇ Read *Strategies on Time Management* and write your own thoughts about this topic.
阅读《时间管理策略》,并写出你的观点。

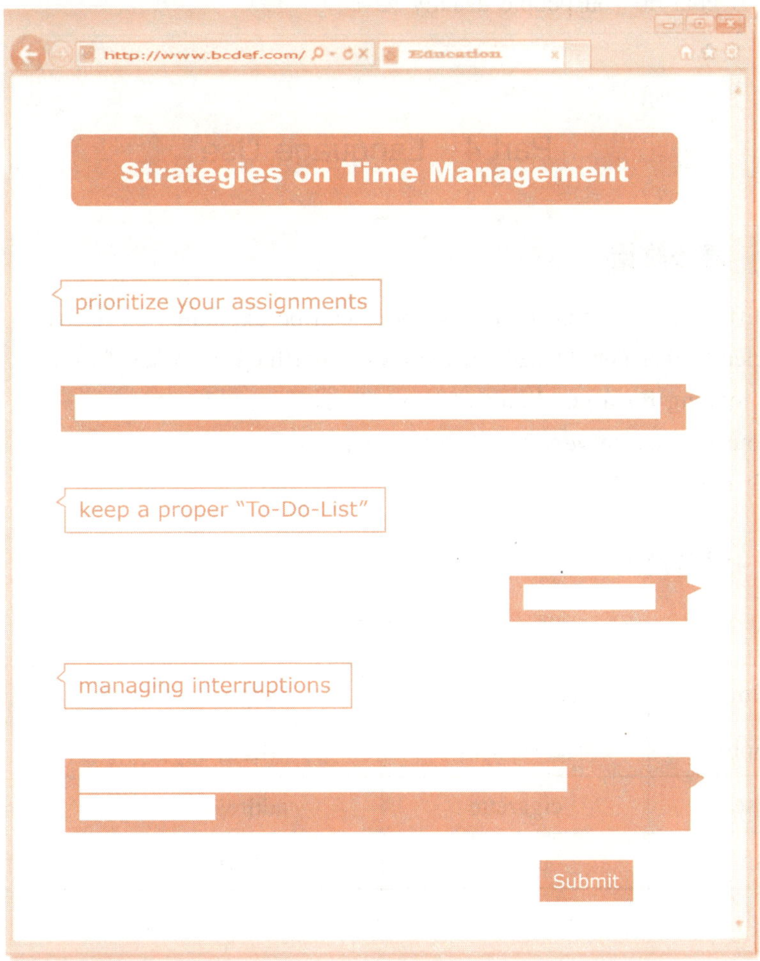

Module 2　Debate & Discussion

Debate: Work in two teams and debate. You have two minutes to think about what you are going to say. 分2组，围绕以下话题，进行辩论。(准备时间:2分钟)

Are we less polite with members of our families than with people we don't know?

Team A	Team B
Opinion 1 ______	Opinion 1 ______
Opinion 2 ______	Opinion 2 ______
Opinion 3 ______	Opinion 3 ______

Discussion: Discuss and answer the question below. 讨论以下话题。

What kinds of goal do you people usually have?

Part 4　Language Use

Module 1　语法改错

1. The difference between the two theories can be explained quite easy.
2. It is clearly that people without money do not have as much freedom.
3. He is looking for a good pair of sport shoes.
4. Eco-tourism can be very benefit to poor areas.
5. I don't understand where the library is.

Module 2　语音练习

Direction: mark the stress within the words below. 标出下列单词的重音。

interesting	atmosphere	hospital	company
photography	newspaper	entertain	employee
Japanese	cigarette	address	translate
mistake	unreal	record	fifteen

Chapter 10 套题练习

套题练习 1

Part 1

1. What work do you do?
2. Why did you choose to do that type of work (or, that job)?
3. Do you like your job?
4. Is it very interesting?
5. (Possibly) Do you miss being a student?

1. What subject(s) are you studying?
2. Why did you choose to study that subject? /Why did you choose to study those subjects?
3. Do you like your subject? (Why? /Why not?)
4. Is it very interesting?
5. (Possibly) Are you looking forward to working?

1. What kind of housing/accommodation do you live in?
2. Do you live in a house or a flat?
3. Who do you live with?
4. How long have you lived there?
5. Do you plan to live there for a long time?

1. What's (the name of) your hometown?
2. Is that a big city or a small place?
3. Please describe your hometown a little.
4. How long have you been living there?
5. Do you like your hometown?

Part 2

Describe a problem that affects the environment in the area where you live.
You should say:
what the problem is
what causes it
what people feel about the problem
and explain what you think could be done to solve it.

Part 3

1. Tell me, what do you think are the greatest problems facing your country at present?
2. And what has been done so far to solve these problems?
3. How successful would you say these measures have been?
4. Do you think things are likely to get better or worse in the future?
5. Is what you are going to study likely to be of any use to solve these problems?
6. Are people concerned about environmental problems in your country?
7. What can individuals do to help?
8. Do you think older people have as much awareness of environmental problems as the younger generation?
9. Do you believe that climate change is a serious problem?
10. Do you think recycling is important?

套题练习 2

Part 1

1. Do you like looking at the sky? Why?
2. In which room of your home can you best see the sky?
3. What is the sky like in your hometown?
4. Do you prefer sky during the day or night?
5. Did you learn anything about stars and planets in school?

1. Do you use letters or emails?
2. Do you prefer to write letters by hands or to use a computer?
3. Which do you more often write, emails or letters?

4. How often do you write an email or letter?
5. What do you usually write about?

1. Are you good at organizing time?
2. How do you organize your time?
3. Why do you organize your time?
4. Do you think planning is important for time management?
5. Would you say you are good at managing in your time?

1. Are weekends important to you?
2. How do you (usually) spend the weekends?
3. Which do you prefer, Saturday or Sunday? (Why?)
4. What do you usually do on the day?
5. Are your weekends today more interesting than your weekends when you were a child?

Part 2

Describe an interesting historic place.
You should say:
what it is
where it is located
what you can see there now
and explain why this place is interesting

Part 3

1. How do people in your country feel about protecting historic buildings?
2. Do you think an area can benefit from having an interesting historic place locally? In what way?
3. Why are historic buildings and monuments important to a city?
4. What do you think will happen to historic places or buildings in the future? Why?
5. Is it better to keep old buildings, or build new modern ones?
6. Do you have an opinion about whether governments should protect old buildings?
7. How were you taught history when you were at school?
8. Are there other ways people can learn about history, apart from at school? How?
9. What do you think we can learn by studying events of the past?
10. Do you think history will still be a school subject in the future? Why?

套题练习 3

Part 1

1. Do you often like to listen to music?
2. When do you listen to music?
3. How much time do you usually spend to listening to music every day?
4. Do you like music?
5. What kind of music do you like to listen to? Why?

1. Are there many (or, any) museums in your hometown?
2. Do you think museums are useful for visitors to your hometown/country?
3. Do you often visit a museum?
4. Did you go to any museums when you were a child?
5. When was the last time you visited a museum?

1. What public holidays do you have in your country?
2. Do people in your country celebrate Christmas?
3. Do you like public holidays?
4. Which public holidays do you like the most?
5. What did you do during the last public holiday?

1. Do you have a favorite teacher?
2. Why do you like the teacher?
3. What kind of teacher do you like?
4. Do you think teachers should be angry to students or not?
5. Do you like strict teachers?

Part 2

Describe a teacher who has influenced you in your education.
You should say:
where you met him/her
what subject he/she taught
what was special about him/her
and explain why this person influenced you so much

Part 3

1. How has education changed in your country in the last 10 years?
2. What changes do you foresee in the next 50 years?
3. Is the Internet a valuable educational tool?
4. What role do you think extracurricular activities play in education?
5. What method of learning works best for you?
6. How beneficial do you think it is to group students according to their level of ability?
7. How are education priorities today different from those in the past?
8. What is your opinion on the way languages are taught in schools?
9. How can the type of school you go to affect career success?
10. What changes do you think will happen in the classroom in the near future?

套题练习 4

Part 1

1. How many hours do you sleep every day?
2. Is it necessary to take a nap every day?
3. Do old people sleep a lot? Why?
4. How to have a good sleep?
5. Do you like to get up early in the morning?

1. What's the most popular means of transport in your hometown?
2. How often do you take buses?
3. Can you compare advantages of planes and trains?
4. Is driving to work popular in your country?
5. Do you think people will drive more in the future?

1. What colors do you like?
2. What's the most popular color in China?
3. Do you like to wear clothes of bright colors?
4. What are the differences between men and women's preference on colors?
5. Do colors affect your mood?

1. What kinds of snacks do you like to eat?
2. Is it healthy to eat snacks?

3. Do your parents allow you to eat snacks?
4. What was the most popular snack when you were young?
5. What kinds of snacks do children in your country like to eat nowadays?

Part 2

Describe something you own which is very important to you.
You should say:
where you got it from
how long you have had it
what you use it for
and explain why it is so important to you.

Part 3

1. What kind of possessions show status in your country?
2. Modern society is often called "materialistic". Why do you think this is?
3. Do you think consumerism is a positive or a negative development?
4. What is the role of advertising?
5. How do you think the Internet will affect buying patterns in the future?
6. What are the main differences between small stores and big stores when you go shopping?
7. Do you think small stores will disappear in the future?
8. What do you think is the best way to advertise?
9. What are the differences between men and women when they go shopping?
10. What do you think of on-line shopping?

Answer

Chapter 2

◇ Exercise 1. Make the following into sentences and read the sentences aloud. 用下列单词组成句子并大声朗读。

1. I/sophomore/plan to/study abroad/master's.

Example: I'm a sophomore student and I'm planning to study abroad for my master's.

2. His salary is relatively decent among his peers.
3. I don't like my school coz our workload is way too heavy.
4. The orientation will be held in the hall tomorrow and everyone is attending.
5. Her presentation focused on a brand-new field which really inspired me.

Module 1 Connectives 连接词

Reason & result

Join the first part of a sentence in the left-hand column with a second part from the right-hand column, using an appropriate expression showing reason or result from the central column. In some cases, more than one of the expressions from the middle is possible.

1. The police asked him his ...	... owning to	... pass his exams
2. He failed his exam ...	... so as not to ...	... wake anyone
3. He spent the whole weekend revising ...	... with the aim of ...	... his lack of revision
4. They came in quietly ...	... in order to ...	... poor student attendance
5. The bank manager refused to lend the company more money ...	... due to ...	... its low turnover and poor sales history
6. The school was forced to close ...	... reason for ...	... speeding through the town

The police asked him reason for speeding through the town.

He failed his exam due to his lack of revision.

He spent the whole weekend revising in order to pass his exams.

They came in quietly so as not to wake anyone.

The bank manager refused to lend the company more money owning to its low turnover and poor sales history.

The school was forced to close owning to poor student attendance.

◇ Write down the synonyms of the following words and describe the word to your group members. 写出下列单词的同义词，并用自己话向身边的同学描述这个单词。

Example: hard: tricky, difficult, frustrating, tough, challenging

✓ something not easy and may require a lot of efforts

[iː]	[i]	[ə]
keep, mean	lip, study, live, assist, diligent, discipline	work, contribute, attention
[ai]	[æ]	
life, white, assignment, biology	laugh, active, math	walk

interesting: fascinating, impressive

✓ arousing a feeling of interest

smart: cleaver, intelligent

✓ having or showing quick intelligence

teacher: tutor, professor, mentor

People who provide you with guidance and help in academic studies

lesson: class, lecture, seminar, tutorial

✓ something to be learned or studied

Part 3 Language Use

Module 1 语法改错

1. My sister is a workaholic. She often works overtime.
2. She loves cats.
3. My grandfather was a fireman. He has retired since last year.
4. We talked about whether universities should charge tuition fees.
5. There are three main reasons for this change.

Module 2 语音练习

Direction: match words with correspondent phonetic according to the underline alphabet. 根据划线的字母将单词填入相对应的音标方框中。

Chapter 3

◇ Exercise 1. Make the following into sentences and read the sentences aloud. 用下列单词组成句子并大声朗读。

1. I/used to/live/granny/childhood.

Example: I used to live with my granny in my childhood.

2. I/remember/day/we first/met/library.

I still remember the day when we first met in the library.

3. Moody/affect/others/around you/colleagues/friends.

Being moody affects others around you such as your colleagues and friends.

4. Friendship/mean/a lot/me/I/believe/it/lays/foundation/many/our relationships.

Friendship means a lot to me because I believe it lays the foundation for many of our relationships.

5. Mark Zuckerburg/who/made/efforts/education/role model/young.

Mark Zuckerburg who made efforts on education is a role model for the young.

Module 1 Connectives 连接词

Give examples

Underline the connectives in the sentences and replace them with the following phrases. 下划线划出每句中代表“举例子”的连接词，并用方框内补充的词组连接词替换写句子。

for instance	like	and things like that
in some cases . . .	take myself as an example	

1. He taught us not only a subject, but also how to carry on learning about the subject after class. For example, he said that we should always try to keep an enquiring and open mind.

He taught us not only a subject, but also how to carry on learning about the subject after class. For instance, he said that we should always try to keep an enquiring and open mind.

2. You can't tell many things just from the appearance, such as the past, hobbies, eating habits and so on.

You can't tell many things just from the appearance, like the past, hobbies, eating habits and so on.

3. The Internet provides people with entertainment, such as watching movie, chatting room and even shopping.

The Internet provides people with entertainment, like watching movie, chatting room and even shopping.

4. Steve is a huge fan of online shopping while I'm not that into it, like I could only do online shopping once a month.

Steve is a huge fan of online shopping while I'm not that into it, take myself as an example I could only do online shopping once a month.

5. Sometimes staying with friends is more relaxing than staying with family.

In some cases, staying with friends is more relaxing than staying with family.

Module 2　Paraphrase 词群同义转换

◇ Write down the synonyms of the following words and describe the word to your group members. 写出下列单词的同义词，并用自己话向身边的同学描述这个单词。

Example：responsibility：obligation，duty，liability

✓ something not easy and may require a lot of efforts

like（喜欢）：be into . . . ，be keen on . . . ，be a huge fan of . . .

✓ to regard with favor

enjoyment：pastime，recreation，entertainment

✓ a particular form or source of pleasure

outgoing：energetic，active，open-hearted，sociable ，friendly

✓ interested in and responsive to others

kind（友善的）：nice，understanding，sweet，lovely，gentle

✓ of a good or benevolent nature or disposition，as a person

Part 3　Language Use

Module 1　语法改错

1. I used to go swimming in the river when I lived in the countryside.
2. You can download movies and store it on your computer.
3. Many articles on this topic are available on the internet.
4. People should act according to what they believe.
5. There is an oak tree in my garden.

Module 2　语音练习

Direction：match words with correspondent phonetic according to the underline alphabet. 根据划线的字母将单词填入相对应的音标方框中。

[θ]	[ð]	[s]
think，thought	there，they，this	sink，say
[v]	[w]	
very，various，university	where，white，wage，always	

Chapter 4

◇ Exercise 1. Make the following into sentences and read the sentences aloud. 用下列单词组成句子并大声朗读。

1. I/try/hiking/as/often/possible.

I try to go hiking as often as possible.

2. As/high-school/student/there/not/much/I/do/change/my/daily routine.

As a high school student，there is not much that I can do to change my daily routine.

3. Ping-pong/no longer/popular/in China，and I remember/used to/play/all the time/

when/I/kid.

Ping-pong is no longer popular in China, and I remember I used to play it all the time when I was a kid.

4. City/colleges/educational attractions/museums and zoos.

In big cities there are many colleges and educational attraction, such as museums and zoos.

5. Weekends/a great time/practice/healthy behaviors/you/have/more time/to do.

In fact, weekends are a great time to practice healthy behaviors because you usually have more time to do so.

Module 1 Connectives 连接词

Contrast and Comparison

Fill in the gaps with words or phrases in the form. 用方框里相应的连接词或词组填空。

1. Tom is always indifferent towards everything, similarly, he doesn't want to depend upon others.
2. Ben wants to be a reporter. On the other hand, he also thinks he would make a fine chef.
3. But at least some people find it equally useful to have the negative pointed out and explained.
4. Most people do not seem to see family business in the same way that they see other jobs.
5. Alternatively, you can register online and enjoy hundreds of movies at home.
6. Instead of doing outdoor sports he prefers painting and other indoor activities.
7. Penny suggested going hiking, however, no one agreed on that.

◇ Write down the synonyms of the following words and describe the word to your group members. 写出下列单词的同义词,并用自己话向身边的同学描述这个单词。

Example: schedule: plan, timetable, a to-do list, arrangement

✓ a plan that lists all the work that you have to do and when you must do each thing

healthy: nutritious , well-being, beneficial

✓ possessing or enjoying good health

relax: release pressure, take a break, rest

✓ to release or bring relief

hobby: interest, specialty

✓ an activity or interest pursued for pleasure

popular: fashionable, trendy, leading

suited to the general masses of people

Part 4 Language Use

Module 1 语法改错

1. My cousin watches TV for 8 hours every day.

2. The government spent ten million dollars on public transport last year.

3. The students who are studying AP Spanish should see me today.

4. I need to find someone who/that can play the piano for our assembly next month.

5. People who/that work with sick and elderly people must be very patient and kind.

Module 2 语音练习

Direction: link the words with a " ~ " and read aloud. 根据连读规律,连接单词并朗读句子。

Nice to meet ~ you.

I'd like another bow(l o)f rice.

I'm ~ an ~ English boy.

Put ~ it ~ on, please.

Did ~ you get there late ~ again?

It ~ is ~ an ~ old book.

Let me have ~ a look ~ at ~ it.

I called ~ you half ~ an ~ hour ~ ago.

Not ~ at ~ all.

Please pick ~ it ~ up.

Would ~ you like ~ a cup ~ of tea?

Can he do it?

Tell him to ask her . . .

Thank ~ you

Could ~ you help me, please?

Chapter 5

◇ Exercise 1. Make the following into sentences and read the sentences aloud. 用下列单词组成句子并大声朗读。

1. My mobile phone/features/text messaging/games/video calls.

My mobile phone has a lot of features like text messaging, games, camera and even video calls.

2. I/fan/comedies/I/love/everything/laugh.

I'm a huge fan of comedies because I love everything that makes me laugh.

3. I/prefer/movies/in the cinema/it/offer me/audio and visual enjoyment/special effects.

I would prefer to watch movies in the cinema because it offers me fantastic audio and visual enjoyment as well as fabulous special effects.

4. Computer/become/my daily life/it/hard/imagine/how/I/survive without it.

Computer has practically become my daily life and it is very hard to imagine how I can survive without it.

5. Although you/turn mobile phone/mute mode, it/distract/you/classes/reduce/

efficiency.

Although you may turn your mobile phone into the mute mode, it will distract you from classes and reduce your study efficiency.

直击考点

Module 1　Connectives 连接词

1. We went out **despite/in spite of** the rain.
2. We went out **though** it was raining.
3. The judge sent her to prison **despite** the fact that she had very small children.
4. **Though** I didn't enjoy the movie, I watched it.
5. I enjoyed the party **though** I didn't know anybody there.
6. I bought the watch, **though** it was expensive.
7. John didn't come; **however**, everybody else did.
8. **Although** the government refuses to admit it, it has failed to revive the economy.
9. He failed **in spite of** his hard work.
10. I didn't like her rude behavior. **However**, I said nothing.

Module 2　Paraphrase 词群同义转换

◇ Write down the synonyms of the following words and describe the word to your group members. 写出下列单词的同义词,并用自己话向身边的同学描述这个单词。

Example: impact: influence

✓ have an effect upon

important: essential, influential, crucial

✓ mattering much

funny: hilarious, humorous, amusing

✓ providing fun

expensive: costly, pricy, high-priced

✓ something not cheap

modern: contemporary, current, the latest

✓ something in recent time

Part 4　Language Use

Module 1　语法改错

1. The number of women studying physics increased dramatically last year.
2. I don't have much time to complete my homework.
3. These days, more and more people travel to foreign countries for their holidays.
4. I hope it is not too late to save endangered animals.
5. There is a pan of porridge and there are some bowls in the kitchen.

Module 2　语音练习

Direction: link the words with a "～" and read aloud. 根据连读规律,连接单词并朗读句子。

Where ～ are your brother ～ and sister?

I ~ ama student.

She wants to study ~ English.

The question is too ~ easy for him to answer.

Is ~ ita ~ hat or a cat?

She can't carry ~ it.

There ~ is ~ a good book in my desk.

She opened the door and walked ~ in.

I looked for ~ it here ~ and there.

There ~ is a football under ~ it.

Shall we meet at ~ eight or ten tomorrow morning?

Here ~ are four ~ eggs.

But where ~ is my cup?

Chapter 6

◇ Exercise 1. Make the following into sentences and read the sentences aloud. 用下列单词组成句子并大声朗读。

1. Congest/become/a daily frustration/urban centers/grow.

Congestion becomes a daily frustration as urban centers are growing.

2. We/comply/a list of/NYC's coolest secret spot, ones/you're/not/likely/read about/in guidebooks.

We've compiled a list of New York City's coolest secret spots, ones you're not likely to read about in any guidebooks.

3. There/an abundance of/park and garden/close to/the CBD/a variety of common and rare species.

There is an abundance of parks and gardens close to the CBD with a variety of common and rare plant species.

4. Most of us/busy/these days/we/hardly/have the time/enjoy/simple things in life.

Most of us are all so busy these days we hardly have the time to enjoy the simple things in life anymore.

5. Smog/hang over/city/is/the most familiar and obvious form/air pollution.

Smog hanging over city is the most familiar and obvious form of air pollution.

直击考点

Module 1 Connectives 连接词

Insert the following connectives into the sentences to make them more logical and coherent. 将下列连接词插入句子中使句子更加完整连贯。

1. It's a difficult job, I enjoy it, though.

2. I was looking forward to a pleasant journey, unfortunately it turned out a nightmare because of the storm.

3. Many subway stations let you cross the platform to change from one route to another. However, at times trains leave before customers can make the connection

4. The west coast of North Uist, Benbecula and South Uist are dominated by extensive areas of white-sanded beaches. In contrast the east coasts of North and South Uist have a mix of extensive moorland, hills and long narrow sea lochs.

5. The weather reports said it's gonna be boiling hot in the next few days, we were excited about going on a road trip still.

6. Beijing is so large that visitors might find it a bit annoying to travel from one destination to another. Nevertheless, public transport will get you to most of the main tourist sites.

7. My flight was delayed to the late evening. Nobody came to explain to us, though.

Module 2 Paraphrase 词群同义转换

◇ Write down the synonyms of the following words and describe the word to your group members. 写出下列单词的同义词,并用自己话向身边的同学描述这个单词。

Example: underground: tube, subway, metro

✓ an underground electric railroad

kind(种类): type, sort

✓ a class or group of individual objects

quiet: peaceful, silent,

✓ making no noise or sound

a lot of: a great deal of, a bunch of, plenty of

✓ a relatively large amount of stuff

safe: secure

✓ free from hurt, injury, danger, or risk

Part 4 Language Use

Module 1 语法改错

1. Why do you think this?
2. I do not agree with her idea.
3. They have been here for three years.
4. If the children are sick, they must stay home and rest.
5. He just managed to avoid hitting the car in front of him.

Module 2 语音练习

Direction: cross the letters that you don't need to pronounce. 将不发音的字母划掉。

Example: The girl in the red coat was on a black bike just now.

1. We're going to work on a farm next Tuesday.
2. I bought a cheap book, but it's a good book.
3. — Do you know his bike number?

— Sorry, I don't know.

4. The big bus from the factory is full of people.
5. What would you like, hot tea or black coffee?
6. I went there alone at nine last night.
7. It's a very cold day, but it's a good day.

Chapter 7

◇ Exercise 1. Make the following into sentences and read the sentences aloud. 用下列单词组成句子并大声朗读。

1. My hometown/a small-sized coastal city/the north of China/therefore/people/a slow-paced life/enjoy/seafood.

My hometown is a small-sized coastal city in the north of China, therefore, people can lead a slow-paced life and enjoy tasty seafood.

2. They/give/hand/visitors/in need/make/feel/at home.

They love to give a hand to the visitors who are in need and make them feel at home.

3. It/been/my dream/go travelling/in Italy/enjoy the breathtaking view/Venice.

It has always been my dream to go travelling in Italy, enjoying the breathtaking view at Venice.

4. The apartment/I/in now/locate/the city center/a bunch of/cool diners and convenient shops/nearby.

The apartment that I live in now is located in the city center with a bunch of cool diners and convenient shops nearby.

5. The place/well-decorated/with/paintings/hang on the walls/amazing chandeliers.

The place is well-decorated, with paintings hanging on the walls, amazing chandeliers.

Module 1 Connectives 连接词递进

Underline the connectives in the following sentences and replace them with the words and phrases in the box. 划出下列例句中的连接词,并用方框里的连接词做替换练习。

another thing is	besides	...., as well	at the same time

1. Perth is famous for its unique landscape. In addition, it has the finest harbor in west Australia.

2. Doing housework always drives me crazy, plus I don't really live in the house that often anymore, which makes me feel even more useless wiping and cleaning stuff.

3. Every visitor enjoys the tropical view in my hometown, what's more the coastal activities like beach volleyball are really attracting for young people.

◇ Write down the synonyms of the following words and describe the word to your group members. 写出下列单词的同义词,并用自己话向身边的同学描述这个单词。

Example: trip: tour, journey

✓ travel to another place

beautiful(形容地点): eye-catching, attractive, spectacular

✓ a place with enjoyable scenery

adapt: get used to

✓ to adjust oneself to different conditions, environment

amazing: wonderful, brilliant, perfect

✓ causing great surprise or sudden wonder

familiar: ordinary, usual, normal

✓ commonly or generally known or seen

Part 4 Language Use

Module 1 语法改错

1. We've spent about $500 buying food for the party.
2. I look forward to hearing your reply soon.
3. New students often feel shy talking to foreign teachers.
4. We're not allowed to skateboard in the park.
5. He lost the race because he had to stop to tie his shoelace.

Module 2 语音练习

Direction: mark the words with the pronunciation rule you leaned today. 划出具有同化发音规则的单词并朗读以下句子。

It's raining cats and dogs.

He stopped reading and looked up.

"On my way home, I looked up an old friend of mine."

He pulled a tired smile when he stepped out of the room.

Before I eat dinner, I read the newspaper for a while.

We read the newspaper every morning.

A: He is not the man he used to be.

B: Don't worry. You'll get used to it in no time.

We used to go there every year.

Our company used to do business with theirs.

Chapter 8

◇ Exercise 1. Make the following into sentences and read the sentences aloud. 用下列单词组成句子并大声朗读。

1. She/taking exercises/lose weight/from day to day.

She has been taking exercises to lose weight from day to day.

2. Chinese children/like/buy many firecrackers/the Spring Festival.

Chinese children like to buy many firecrackers before the Spring Festival.

3. I'm/consider/buy/a second-hand computer/I/short/money now.

I'm considering buying a second-hand computer for I'm short of money now.

4. In my opinion/ability/painting/depend/mainly/talents.

In my opinion, the ability of painting depends mainly on talents.

5. I believe/it's/young/are/passionate about celebrating Christmas/than/old are.

I believe it's the young who are more passionate about celebrating Christmas than the old are.

Module 1 Connectives 连接词强调

Underline the connectives in the following sentences and the replace them with the words and phrases in the box. 划出下列例句中的连接词,并用方框里的连接词做替换练习。

1. She was very fond of speaking French, which indeed she spoke well.

actually

2. He will of course say yes to my proposal.

undoubtedly

3. Most importantly, you must work hard to catch up.

The thing is

4. I know, but I like canned fruit, especially canned pineapple.

In particular

surely	undoubtedly	the thing is	actually
in particular	absolutely		

Module 2 Paraphrase 词群同义转换

◇ Write down the synonyms of the following words and describe the word to your group members. 写出下列单词的同义词,并用自己话向身边的同学描述这个单词。

Example: delicious: tasty, mouth-watering, savory, appetizing

✓ highly pleasing to the senses, especially to taste or smell

restaurant: diner, eatery

✓ a place to have a meal

unhealthy: bad, stale, mouldy

✓ not in a state of good or normal health

buy: purchase, get, take, pay for

✓ to acquire the possession of

eat: have, enjoy, have a bite

✓ to take a meal

Part 4 Language Use

Module 1 语法改错

1. The woman apologized for standing on my foot.
2. The driver spent a lot of time looking for his car keys.

3. He will start his course in July.
4. In China, the standard of living is much better than in the past.
5. The data was taken from 1960 to 1996.

Module 2　语音练习

Direction: mark the words with the pronunciation rule you leaned today. 划出具有同化发音规则的单词并朗读以下句子。

Now look what a mess you've made.
Do you miss your family?
I shall miss you very much.
Take care that you don't spoil your new clothes.
A: I'm very glad to meet you.
B: It's a pleasure to meet you.
I'm sorry to tell that you've been dismissed.
Would you show me the bathroom, please?
Would you care to go for a walk with me?
Could you do me a favor?
Could you possibly give me a lift home?
She has traveled in northern countries.
The southern half of the country is a desert.
She says help only the worthy poor.
This book is worthy of being read [to be read].

Chapter 9

Part 4　Language Use

Module 1　语法改错

1. The difference between the two theories can be explained quite easily.
2. It is clear that people without money do not have as much freedom.
3. He is looking for a good pair of sports shoes.
4. Eco-tourism can be very beneficial to poor areas.
5. I don't know where the library is.

Module 2　语音练习

Direction: mark the stress within the words below. 标出下列单词的重音。

'interesting	'atmosphere	'hospital	'company
pho'tography	'newspaper	enter'tain	employ'ee
Japa'nese	ciga'rette	a'ddress	trans'late
mis'take	un'real	record	fif'teen